SOME SLAVES OF RAPPAHANNOCK COUNTY, VIRGINIA

Will Books A to D, 1833–1865
and Old Rappahannock
County, Virginia,
Will Books 1 and 2, 1664–1682

Compiled by

Sandra Barlau

HERITAGE BOOKS
2018

HERITAGE BOOKS
AN IMPRINT OF HERITAGE BOOKS, INC.

Books, CDs, and more—Worldwide

For our listing of thousands of titles see our website at
www.HeritageBooks.com

Published 2018 by
HERITAGE BOOKS, INC.
Publishing Division
5810 Ruatan Street
Berwyn Heights, Md. 20740

Copyright © 2018 Sandra Barlau

Heritage Books by the author:

Some Slaves of Fauquier County, Virginia, Volume I: Will Books 1–10, 1759–1829
Some Slaves of Fauquier County, Virginia; Volume II: Will Books 11–20, 1829–1847
Some Slaves of Fauquier County, Virginia, Volume III: Will Books 21–31, 1847–1869
Some Slaves of Fauquier County, Virginia; Volume IV: Master Index, Will Books 1–31, 1759–1869
Some Slaves of Rappahannock County, Virginia, Will Books A to D, 1833–1865 and Old Rappahannock County, Virginia, Will Books 1 and 2, 1664–1682

Cover portrait: Mary Timbers Harrison

All rights reserved. No part of this book may be reproduced or transmitted in any form or by any means, electronic or mechanical, including photocopying, recording or by any information storage and retrieval system without written permission from the author, except for the inclusion of brief quotations in a review.

International Standard Book Numbers
Paperbound: 978-0-7884-5860-6

TABLE OF CONTENTS

RAPPAHANNOCK COUNTY, VA

PREFACE v

INTRODUCTION vii

ABBREVIATIONS ix

WILL BOOK A 1

    1833-1842 1

WILL BOOK B 17

    1842-1849 17

WILL BOOK C 33

    1849-1855 33

WILL BOOK D 49

    1855-1865 49

OLD RAPPAHANNOCK COUNTY, VA

WILL BOOK 1 63

    1665 - 1677 63

WILL BOOK 2 65

    1677 – 1682 65

INDEX 69

PREFACE

The idea for this book originated after I had compiled the Fauquier County Virginia Will Books 1-31 from 1759 to 1869. I wanted to find the mother of my 2nd gr-grandmother Mildred. I think I found her.

This time I am looking for an ancestor of my gr-grandmother Kitty Gaines. She and a descendent of Elvira Gaines, Lucy Gaines Grigsby, look enough alike to be sisters. The question now is – are they related and if so, how?

INTRODUCTION

Will Books are a good source in the search for slaves only if the owner named the slave(s). Many times a Will lists property without specifying if it includes slaves. For example: "I will and bequeath to my (wife, son, daughter, etc.) all my estate both real and personal of every sort." or "...the property I have already given to my (wife, son, daughter, etc.)..." The documents often do not include the slave's name, sometimes only girl, runaway, boy, etc.

Each chapter is one Will Book. The documents include Administrator's Estate, Executor and Guardian Accounts, Wills, Inventory and Appraisals. Each slave owner is listed first followed by the page number, date and type of document. The list of slaves follows below. The new owner is listed if known. Surnames of the owner's children are indexed only if noted in the document. The slaves who were emancipated, freed or manumitted are listed in the index under Emancipated.

Not included in this summary is a slave's monetary value, if the slave was sold, hired by the estate, hired out or who hired the slave. The original text should be read to determine which occurred. Sometimes the estate or guardian account listed people paying money to the estate but not why the remittances were paid.

First names were standardized in order to make your index search easier. When you go to the original Will Books be aware that different spellings were used. Be creative in looking for first names: Sharlot (Charlotte), Ausker (Oscar), Fillis (Phillis), etc. Sometimes the written nn could be rr and many times S resembles L. Some of the entries have only a few letters separated with a blank space such as Marj__i_.

It would be a good idea to peruse the entire index. You may recognize a name under another spelling. The same name can also appear more than once on a page under different owners.

It is important to note the slave's age since the value of a slave increases or decreases with age and ability. It can also be used as a tracking tool.

Some of the microfilmed pages are very faint. The quality of the films varies and some microfilm copies were difficult to read. There were many guesses as to the written names and I take full responsibility for any errors in transcription.

The Will Books read for this volume are on microfilm held by the Family History Library at Salt Lake City. They are also available on-line through Family History Centers.

I hope this book helps you to locate a slave or an owner. Good luck in your search.

ABBREVIATIONS

adm acct – Administrator's Account

exec acct – Executor Account

gdn acct – Guardian Account

inv & appr – Inventory & Appraisal

div – Division (of slaves, land, property)

comm acct – Committee Account

WILL BOOK A
1833-1842

Mary JORDAN .... pg 1, 19 Sept 1829, will

    girl Caroline to niece Sarah G. JORDAN

Alcy NORMAN .... pg 8, 8 June 1833, will

    man Edmond to husband Thomas NORMAN, if he outlives my husband he is to be free

Thomas HUGHES .... pg 10, 2 Oct 833, inv & appr

    old man Joe, Mary & 2 children Nelson & Daniel, woman Sucky, old man Jim, men Isaac, Reuben, Absalom, Henry, woman Betty

John CUREE .... pg 12, 31 Aug 1833, inv & appr

    women Dinah, Jinny, Milly, Hannah, young man George, boys Jordan, Moses, Adam, Sam, Amanda & child Dawson, woman Kitty, Fillis (Phyllis) & child Wesley, boys Frederick, Martin, girls Delila, Charlotte, Jam, Martha, boy Sanford, Mald & child ___, boys Eldridge, William, _illis, Manuel, men Bird, Robinson, Anthony, Clary & child ___, woman Ann

Jane THORNTON .... pg 14, 1 Oct 1833, will

    1/4 equal part of slaves to grandson Alfred A. THORNTON; 1/4 equal part of slaves to grandsons George W. THORNTON & Aylell H. THORNTON; remaining ¼ part to granddaughter Caroline H. THOMPSON; Lucy & her daughter Sally to granddaughter Mary Frances THORNTON; girl Hannah, Lydia the daughter of Lucy to granddaughter Elizabeth A.T. THORNTON

Aylett HAWES .... pg 16, 9 Aug 1832, will

    those who are old & infirm to choose place of residence with any of my relations; old & infirm Jack; all slaves to be emancipated - those nearly white as to be unsafe to go to Liberia to Ohio under the patronage of David S. DODY; Cally to choose her patron; all other slaves to Liberia; the superannuated of the negroes to Howard THORNTON until they are removed to Ohio & Liberia; the superannuated of the negroes in Caroline to Walker HAWES

William FARROW .... pg 25, 2 Jan 1834, inv & appr

men Sam, Jess, old woman Hannah

Frederick DUNCAN .... pg 31, 3 Feb 1834, div of slaves

James, woman Nancy, Felissa & her child Ellen, Manu to Susannah DUNCAN widow; boy Charles to Edmond _. DUNCAN; girl Amelia to Eldridge DUNCAN; girl Helen to James M. DUNCAN; man Thornton to Frederick DUNCAN; girls Evelene, Hannah to Harrison DUNCAN; Isaac, Harriet to Mary Ann DUNCAN; Elizabeth, Daniel to Randolph DUNCAN

Frederick DUNCAN .... pg 32, 23 Dec 1833, inv & appr

men James, Thornton, Isaac, girl Nancy, Felissa & her child Ellen, girl Helen, boy Charles, girls Elizabeth, Eveline, Harriet, boy Daniel, girl Hannah, old woman Nancy, girl Amelia

James WITHERS Jr. .... pg 35, 23 Dec 1833, inv & appr

James age 21, Austin 21, Jerry 30, Thornton 32, Sary 48, Silvey 35, Alecy 25, Jared 3, Hannah 5, Tompson 11, Narassa 11, Amy 11, Frances 6, Vincent 13, Ely 11, Henry 9

Bird EASTHAM .... pg 36, 11 Feb 1834, inv & appr

Moses age 40, Delila 20, Albert 19, Charles 17, Washington 12, David 13, Armistead 23, Daniel 14, Enoch 9, Charlotte 32, Rebecca 19 & children Ellen & Jane, Sophia 25 & children French & Ellen, Julia Ann 8, Elizabeth 9, Clary 37, James 17, Cassy 14, Gilbert 11, Samuel 8, Reuben 43, Tanner, Henry, Thomas 34, Edmund 31, Randol 47, Coleman 9, Humphrey 33, Maria 37 & child Lucy, Maria 37, Squire 6, Jude 21 & child Baylor

William FARROW..................................pg 42, 2 Jan 1834, list of sales

woman Hannah to Elizabeth SIMPSON; man Jesse to Elijah BAINES; man Sam to French FARROW

Thomas HUGHES..................pg 44, 12 May 1834, acct of sales

boy Isaac to George EGGBORN; Mary & 2 children; Joe, Susan, woman Betty, man Absalom to Boneman HUGHES; men Reuben, Jim, Henry to Thomas WALDEN

Aylett HAWES.................................. pg 48, 12 May 1834, inv & appr

Benjamin Johnson, Nully, Elena, Gabriel, Mary, Margaret, Nelly, Aylett, Judy Sanford, Frances, Jack Harris, Fanny, Charles, Milton, Sandy, Moses, Jeffrey, Betsy, Philip, Lucy Brent, Richard, Henrietta, Letty, Charlotte, Malary, Austin, Warrenton, Rosanna Jones, Lucy Ann, Richard Davis, Phoebe, Esther Zoliver, Frank, Celia, John, George, Samuel, Keller, Matilda, Henry, Maria, John R. Gordon, Prudence, Marshall, Nat, Aaron P. Davis, Belinda, Charles Gray, Jane, James, Lewis Jones, Lavina, Patty, Charlotte, Belinda, Jane, Bob Gevin, J__y, Ellen, Lewis Rickson, Joseph Gerdan, Letty, David Madison, Winney Campbell, Sally Walker, Isaac, Andrew, Hannah, Nancy, Eliza, Tom Toliver, Ivy, Reuben Mason, William Whiting, Gardner B_mkin, Walker, Rachel, John Gordan

Sarah HAYNIE .... pg 56, 8 Sept 1834, inv & appr

woman & child, boy French, girls Milly, Harriet, Adaline

Aylett HAWES.................................. pg 58, 11 Dec 183_, inv & appr

John age 50, Stephen 50, Thornton 18, Ann 15, Louisa 10, Charlotte 18 & infant Susan; Jenny 8, Henry 6, Betty 40 of one family; Lucinda 20 & child James 8 of one family; Nat 20, Polly 30, Eleanor 14, Aylett 12, Robert 10, Walker 8, Nancy 11, Elizabeth 2 of one family; Lilly 30, William 18, Emily 12, Henry 10, Milly 8, Dolly 6, Kitty 2 of one family; Grace 70

John JEFFRIES .... pg 61, 20 June 1834, will

Frank to my 3 children Francis M. JEFFRIES, Jemima JEFFRIES, & Louiza JEFFRIES

George DEATHERAGE .... pg 62, 26 May 1834, inv & appr

woman Celia

Bird EASTHAM ....pg 69, 8 Sept 1834, div of slaves

Moses age 40, Thomas 34, Armistead 25, Reuben 43, Edmond 31, Mariah 37, Squire 7, Lucy 3, Humphrey 33, Clary 37, Cassy 14, Gilbert 11, Samuel 8, Sophia 27 & 2 children, George French 6, Elizabeth 11, Albert 20, Coleman 10, Charlotte 52, Charles 17, Daniel 13, Washington 12, Enoch 100, David 14, Delila 23, Juda 70, Bailer 4, Henry 9

Lot 1: Moses, Elizabeth to Robert EASTHAM; Lot 2: Thomas, Squire, Charlotte to Lawson EASTHAM; Lot 3: Armistead, Cassy to Bird EASTHAM; Lot 4: Edmund, Coleman, Washington to the heirs of Philip EASTHAM dec'd; Lot 5: Reuben Mariah, Delila to John EASTHAM; Lot 6: Humphrey, Juda, Bailer to Thomas HAND; Lot 7: Charles, Sophia & her 2 children to George EASTHAM; Lot 8: Daniel, Gilbert, Samuel to Branton EASTHAM; Lot 9: David, Clary, Henry to Benjamin F. EASTHAM; Lot 10: Albert, Lucy, George French, Enoch to Absalom JORDAN

James WITHERS .... pg 72, 4 Sept 1834, will

Willis, Fielding, Harry, A__, Eve, Charity to wife; Daniel, Mary, Luce, Caroline, Ann, Mahilah, Aby to daughter Alcey wife of John PORTER; Mary, Mime, Caroline, Elias, Reuben, Elijah, Charlotte to daughter Fanny; Kate, Luce, Milly, Jack, Edmund, Mi__, Aaron to daughter Katy; the remainder of slaves not mentioned to be divided between my 3 daughters Fanny, Suckey, & Alcy except Tel & her increase – they are to be divided between Fanny & Katy

Thomas GRIFFIN ....pg 74, 23 Oct 1834, inv & appr

boys William, Henry

Thomas BRAGG .... pg 75, 19 Sept 1833, inv & appr

    man Willis, boys Madison, Thornton, girl Louiza, Jane & her child Mildred, girl Maria

Thomas BRAGG .... pg 75, 20 & 21 Sept 1833, acct of sales

    man Willis, boy Madison, girl Lucinda, boy Thornton, girl Maria to Henry R. MENEFEE; Jane & her child Mildred to John HOPKINS

John JEFFRIES .... pg 80, 5 Dec 1834, inv & appr

    Peter age 60, Hannah 60, man Rigen 35, Alfred 25, Harriet 30 & child John, Lucy 23 & child Sarah, Judy 22 & child Henry, Stephen 10, Thomas 8, Emily 10, Davenport 6, Collin 6, Charles 4, Howard 4, Frank 36

Jane THORNTON .... pg 82, 1 Nov 1833, inv & appr

    women Elizabeth, Isabella, Patsy, Betsy, boy William, women Phillis, Molly, Caty, boy Jacob, men Joshua, Abraham, Edmund, woman Jane, men Prince, Dennis, boy Bob, man Butler, boy John, Keziah & child, women Winney, Katy, man Lewis, woman Lucy & her daughter Sally willed to Mary Frances THORNTON, woman Hannah & Lucy's child Lydia willed to Elizabeth A.T. THORNTON

Louzia JEFFRIES .... pg 87, 15 Oct 1834, will

    Frank to sister Jemima JEFFRIES

Richard GRAY .... pg 89, 23 Mar 1810, will

    girl Fanny to be sold

Frances KENDALL .... pg 92, 22 Jan 1830, will

    Celia, Ruthy, Martha & their present & future increase to wife Melinda KENDALL, to be freed after her death

Thomas FOLEY ....pg 94, 26 Aug 1834, inv & appr

    boy Henry, man Jesse, woman Maria, boys Armistead, Chilton, Burnette, woman Harriet, boys Solomon, Richard, Elias, Franklin, woman & child, boys Simon, Thornton, girl May, man Tom

Leonard BARNES ....pg 102, 31 Mar 1835, inv & appr

    old Joe, old Charlotte, Eleck, Reuben, Willis, Evelene, Mariah & child & children, Jim, Peter, Celia, Phillis, & Nancy; Charlotte Shumate & child & children Edmund, Bob, Early, Walden, & Manda; Horace, Charlotte & child, Mary, George, Lucy, Nelson

Frederick DUNCAN ......pg 105, 24 Dec 1833 – 24 June 1835, estate acct

    James, Nancy, Filliss (Phillis?) & her child Ellen, Maria listed under Susannah DUNCAN widow; boy Charles listed under Edward P. DUNCAN; girl Emily listed under Eldridge G. DUNCAN; man Thornton listed under Frederick DUNCAN; girls Evelina, Hannah listed under Harrison DUNCAN; Isaac, Harriet listed under Mary Ann DUNCAN; Elizabeth, Daniel listed under Randolph DUNCAN

James WITHERS Sr. ....pg 109, 4 July 1835, inv & appr

    Willis, Fielding, Harry, Amy, Eve, Charity, Daniel, Mahala, Abby, Lucy, Caroline, Anne, Mary (dead), Mary, Mime, Caroline, Elias, Reuben, Lige, Charlotte, Cate, Lucy, Milly, Jack, Edward, Miner, Aaron, Abram, Notley, Adam, Menot, Arch, Roy, Joe, Peggy, Hannah, Prince, Ben, Fanny & child Lucy, Mima & child Phil, Dinah, Tell & child George

James WITHERS Sr. .... pg 111, 8 Dec 1834, div of slaves

    Willis, Fielding, Harry, Amy, Eve, Charity to Susan WITHERS widow; Mary, Mime, Caroline, Elias, Reuben, Lige, Charlotte, Roy, Arch, Fanny, Lucy, Diana to Frances WITHERS; Cate, Lucy, Milly, Jack, Edward, Miner, Aaron, Adam, Menor, Hannah, Prince, Ben, Joe to Catherine WITHERS; Daniel, Mahala, Abby, Lucy, Caroline, Ann, Mary, Abram, Notley, Mary, Phil to John PORTER

William DODSON .... pg 112, 24 May 1835, will

    Jesse, Sinah, Jincess, James to brother Samuel DODSON

Aylett HAWES .... pg 113, 19 Mar 1834 – 3 Aug 1835, estate acct

    Tom, negroes moved to Fredericksburg & Liberia

Edward WILLEY .... pg 114, 4 Aug 1835, inv & appr

    Sam age 45, Betty 36, Charles 11

Aylett HAWES .... pg 132, 14 Oct 1833 – 14 Nov 1835, estate acct

    negroes; Charles, Patty

William E. JONES .... pg 135, 22 Oct 1835, inv & appr

    man Sam, boy Meredith, woman Celia, Polly, Fanny, girl Hannah, Eliz, Adaline, Harriet, Kelly, boy Shubel, Washington, Lewis

Moses GIBSON .... pg 144, 26 Apr 1836, will

    negroes of her choosing to wife Elizabeth W. GIBSON

Leonard BARNES .... pg 146, 15 - 16 Sept 1835, acct of sales

    girl Evelina to John R. BROWNING; Charlotte & 2 children to Isham COMWILL; man Willis to David L. JONES; man Reuben to Charles A. THORNTON

Philip EASTHAM .... pg 150, 22 Dec 1836, div of slaves

    Nancy, Washington age 8 to Susan Ann EASTHAM; Edmund 33 to Mary Ann EASTHAM; Coleman 10, Lucy Ann to John _. ADAMS

William DODSON .... pg 151, 23 Sept 1835, inv & appr

    man Jesse, Sinah & child, boys Jincess, James

John JEFFRIES .... pg 152, 8 Aug 1836, estate div

Rison, Lucy, Ellen to Jane JEFFRIES, widow; Emily, Henry, Alfred, Harriet to Frances M. JEFFRIES; Collin, Davenport Howard to Lewis WOOD; Jude, Charles, Oscar to Jemima JEFFRIES; Stephen, Tom to Elias CORDER; negroes left by Louisa JEFFRIES dec'd settled to her will

William DODSON .... pg 156, 2 Nov 1835 – 6 July 1836, adm acct

Jincess sold, man Jesse, boy

George DUNCAN .... pg 157, 17 Sept 1836, inv & appr

man Ben, Lucy, boy Anderson, woman Caroline

Mary CHEEK .... pg 162, 4 Oct 1836, will

girl Rachel to Mary JASPER, daughter of Daniel JASPER & Mildred his wife; man Daniel to Robert JASPER son of Daniel JASPER & Mildred his wife

Mitchell ROBERTSON Sr. .... pg 173, 18 May 1835, will

...at the decease of wife Rose ROBERTSON: Milly, Sabra & her children Frederick & Matilda to daughter Sarah Ann WHITE; Charlotte & her children Rose, Jack, Harrison, & Frederick, Polly & her child Robert, man Jack to daughter Sarah Ann WHITE in trust for son William Mitchell ROBERTSON & wife Elizabeth

Henry GRIGSBY .... pg 181, 28 Nov 1836, inv & appr

women Clary, Nancy, Caty & child Mary, Henry, Nelson, Simon, Allen, Delia, Billy, Jacob, Nancy

George DEATHERAGE ....
.... pg 183, 1 Aug 1836 – 10 June 1837, estate acct

woman Celia during her sickness & burial

Nancy DANIEL .... pg 186, 23 Dec 1836, will
   man London to sister Molly DANIEL

Mary Ann DUNCAN .... pg 187, 1 Sept 1835 – 20 Sept 1837, gdn acct
   man Isaac

Elijah ROBERTSON Sr. .... pg 190, 1 June 1837, will
   Fran, Harris, Deck, French, Louisa to daughter Mary ROBINSON; Hannah, Rose, Gena, John, Ocsilin to granddaughter Martha TURNER; old Venus to live with daughter or granddaughter

John JEFFRIES .... pg 198, 14 Oct 1834 – 7 Oct 1837, exec acct
   Alfred, Harriet sold

John LALE .... pg 203, 20 June 1837, inv & appr
   men Addison, William, boy William, girls Patience, Hannah, men Peter, George, woman, girls Jane, Rachel, boys Stephen, Richard, girl Margaret, boy Sam, girl Jane

George DUNCAN .... pg 209, 28 Sept 1836 – 23 Dec 1837, estate acct
   woman & child sold

John BAURE .... pg 210, 29 Dec 1837, inv & appr
   man Guy, woman Mary, girl Peggy, boy Logan

John SMITH .... pg 214, 29 Dec 1837, inv & appr
   Strother, Judah, Sally, Lucinda, Sarah, Winney

James MENEFEE .... pg 227, 5 Mar 1838, inv & appr
   men Addison, George, Henry, women Rose, Nully, Mary, Ellen, boy Richard, 4 children Teresy, Martha, Arch, Isabella

Thomas JONES.................................. pg 236, 16 Dec, 1836, inv & appr
  Milly

Nancy HAWKINS.............................. pg 240, July 1837, inv & appr
  women Caty, Jenny, girls Matilda, Henrietta

Nancy HAWKINS.............................. pg 241, 3 Apr 1838, acct of sales
  Jane & child hired by Thomas SMITH

James MENEFEE............................... pg 243, 6 Mar 1838, acct of sales
  Henry, George, Rose, Mary, girl Ellen, boy Richard to Tabitha MENEFEE; Nully & children no bids

Susan PRATT..................................... pg 249, 28 Sept 1823, will
  girl Maria to grand niece Susan Elizabeth Ann PRATT daughter of Thomas B. PRATT; man Daniel to nephew William PRATT

James WITHERS Sr........ pg 252, 23 Oct 1835 – 23 June 1838, estate acct
  old Peggy, Sally, Butler

Anthony HAYNIE............................... pg 254, 25 Aug 1838, inv & appr
  Henry age 30, Emanuel 25, Fanny _0, Rachel 22 & child Eliza 8 months, Mary 22 & John 17 months, Rose 6, Robert 4, Somerville 2, Lucinda 7, Matilda 3

Philip N. AMISS .... pg 258, 30 July 1838, inv & appr
  man Billy, boys William, Frank, women Judy, Sarah

John SMITH...................................... pg 267, 18 Jan 1838, acct of sales
  woman Judy, old Winney to Delphia SMITH Sr.; man Strother, woman Sally to William SMITH

Thomas FOLEY............ pg 270, 22 May 1838, inv & appr

    man Tom, boy Solomon, old man Jesse, old woman Harriet, boy Franklin

Susannah STALLARD........pg 275, 27 Mar 1837 – 7 Jan 1839, estate acct

    negroes hired

Reuben JEFFRIES...........pg 284, 25 Nov 1837 – 18 Feb 1839, estate acct

    sale of negroes; boy Columbus, Evelina to Nancy JEFFRIES; girl Frances, Harriet to Celia JEFFRIES; ...paid Nancy JEFFRIES in negroes...paid Rodham JONES in right of his wife in negroes

James MENEFEE.............. pg 288, 14 Feb 1839, acct of sales

    Rose age 52, Ellen 14, Addison 23, Henry 40, Richard 9 to Philip S. MENEFEE; Mary 20, George 60, Letty 68 to Tabitha MENEFEE

Elizabeth FOLEY............pg 288, 20 May 1838 – 18 Mar 1839, adm acct

    Jesse to James FOLEY

Easter Verlinda ADAMS.............................pg 292, 3 Oct 18_7, will

    girl Levina to brother George WILLET & sister Sarah WILLET

Reuben JEFFRIES.............pg 295, 24 Nov 1837, inv & appr

    women Phillis, Caroline, girls Mary, Mandy, boys Turner, Columbus, girls Frances, Harriet, Eveline

Ann PULLER.................pg 296, 20 Feb 1839, will

    boy Daniel Morgan to niece Emily M.A. BOWEN; woman Jenny, boy Jacob to niece Adelene A. SPINDLE in trust of William A. SPINDLE her brother
    .... 2 Mar 1839, codicil

    woman Jenny, boy Jacob to niece Adelene A. SPINDLE

Frank PAYNE .... pg 301, 17 Aug 1837, div of slaves

   James, Washington, Mary, Matilda old woman Violet to widow; Maria & child Richard to Robinson COONES; Tender to George S. PAYNE; James to James STOLLAND; Mary to Frances PAYNE; Jefferson to Alexander PAYNE; Jackson to John PAYNE; Madison to Frances PAYNE; Denise to James PAYNE; Munroe to Patsy PAYNE; Winfried to Samuel PAYNE

Frank PAYNE .... pg 303, 10 July 1838 – 22 Jan 1839, estate acct

   negroe hired

Nancy HAWKINS .... pg 304, 1 Jan 1838 – 5 July 1839, adm acct

   Jane & child, Caty

Thomas THORNHILL .... pg 305, 6 Sept 1839, inv & appr

   men Henry, Abraham, Lewis, Walker, Annake, Milly & her 3 children May Louisa, & Phil, woman Haney, old man Alec

Elizabeth BUTLER .... pg 307, 23 Nov 1835 – 20 Nov 1836, estate acct

   slaves sold

Charles WILLIS .... pg 308, 22 June 1839, inv & appr

   man Ned

John LALE .... pg 314, 1 Nov 1837 – 8 Nov 1839, adm acct

   Jack, girl Jane

Thomas THORNHILL .... pg 319, 9 Dec 1839, acct of sales

   man Walker to Elijah CHEEK; man Henry to Joseph THORNHILL; man N_as, man Aylett to Robert THORNHILL; man Lewis to Benjamin LELLARD; man Abraham to William THORNHILL; woman & 2 children to Burwell K. WOOD; woman Haney to Bryant THORNHILL

James MENEFEE............... pg 327, 14 May 1838 – 1 Jan 1840, adm acct

 slaves sold

Phillip RUDASILL .... pg 333, 3 Mar 1840, inv & appr

 men Ned, George, Wilson, girl Miranda, boy John

Mary GIBSON .... pg 345, 17 Nov 1838, will

 Mary's will has (my negroes excepted) & it looks like property other than the negroes goes to the following daughters. I don't see where she specifically states where the negroes go.

 Mary _ KEITH, Eliza Ann KEITH, Judith KEITH, Louisa T. KEITH, America J. KEITH & Caroline M. KEITH daughters of Judith KEITH & her husband Peyton KEITH

Ann PULLIN.. pg 347, 27 Dec 1839, inv & appr

 man Cupid, women Phillis, Isabella, Jerrett, Thomas, Robert, Jacob, Daniel, Morgan, Jinny

Phillip N. AMISS .... pg 349, 29 May 1838 – 15 July 1840, adm acct

 negroes; boy Bill

William R. JONES .... pg 353, 18 Sept 1833 – 10 Nov 1840, gdn acct

 Stephen

Merryman SETTLE............................. pg 359, 21 May 1839, inv & appr

 men Edmond, John

Diannah SETTLE .... pg 359, 21 May 1839, inv & appr

 woman Annaca

Ephram SETTLE............................ pg 361, 21 May 1839, inv & appr
   man Will

Sandy WATERS .... pg 362, 28 May 1839, inv & appr
   men Tom, Williamson, old Tom, women Jinny, Cassa, Matilda, boys George, Jack, Jim, Edmund, girl Charity Ann, boy blind John

Sandy WATERS .... pg 364, 12 Sept 1839, acct of sales
   woman Cassa to Sandy P. WATERS; girl Cha_t_an; boy James to Winford BLACKWELL; boy George to John WATERS; man Tom, boy Jack to Mortimore WATERS; woman Jinny to Mrs. C. DEATHERAGE

Michael NICOL.......................... pg 368, 22 Dec 1840, inv & appr
   men Edmund, Charles, woman Matilda & 3 children Louis, Malinda, & Ann

Moses GIBSON............................pg 371, 9 Nov 1836, inv & appr
   Levi; woman Sally, Nelly, Lavina, boy Daniel, girl Letty, Robert, Randal, Charles, Robin in possession of widow

Benjamin BASYE ....pg 373, 26 Feb 1841, inv & appr
   man George, Talby & child Bedford, Mary & child Beverly, girls Ellen, Elzina, boys Festus, Matthew, John

Elias FOGG..................... pg 389, 6 Sept 1839 – 24 May 1841, adm acct
   cash paid to Lucus, a free man of color

Sandy WATERS ....pg 391, 28 May 1839 – 1 July 1841, adm acct
   negroes sold

John MILLER Sr. .... pg 395, 16 June 1840, will

>her selection of slaves to wife; slaves on land near Washington & those slaves not chosen by wife to son Franklin MILLER at death of wife chice of 1 slave; slaves to be divided among children Henry, John, Franklin, Elizabeth SETTLE, Lucy WOOD, Eliza JONES, Sarah WHEATLEY, & Polly MILLER after death of wife; remainder of slaves to be sold

Moses GIBSON .... pg 405, 23 Oct 1841, list of sales

>man Levi to Besy YATES; woman Hagar to Miner GIBSON

Rhoda HAYNES .... pg 410, 3 Nov 1841, inv & appr

>men Henry, Manuel, Mary & child, old woman Fanny, girls Lucinda, Rosette, Rachel & child, boy Robert, girls Matilda, Somerville, boy Lewis, girls Eliza, Maria, Emily

William SCOTT .... pg 419, 29 May 1841, inv & appr

>girl Lucinda, man Anthony

William SCOTT .... pg 420, 14 Mar 1842, acct of sales

>girl to James R. NELSON, man to J. BAKER

Vincent TAPP .... pg 423, 25 Feb 1842, inv & appr

>Aggy & 2 children, George 4 years, Edwin 13, Milly 60

Vincent TAPP .... pg 424, 8 Mar 1842, acct of sales

>woman & children to Col. Thomas SPINDLE; boy to James R. NELSON; boy Edwin to Peter B. BOWEN; old woman to Judith TAPP

Ann BUTLER .... pg 427, 27 Dec 1839 – 31 Dec 1841, adm acct

>old negro

David KENNARD .... pg 443, 31 Dec 1840, will

> negroes to be divided among daughters Henrietta & Sarah & the rest of my children

Moses GIBSON .... pg 448, Mar 1835 – 10 Nov 1841, exec acct

> boy West exchanged for bond

Reuben CANNON .... pg 454, 6 Aug 1842, inv & appr

> man Gay, boy Lewis, girl

John MILLER .... pg 456, 11 July 1842, inv & appr

> men John, George, Anthony, Isaac, Thomas, women Phillis, Mary Silvy, boys Alfred, Gabriel, Robert, Sanford, William, Arthur, Books, Lewis, girls Eliza, Harriet, Maria, Ellen, Betsy, Emily

Daniel KINNARD .... pg 459, 22 Aug 1842, inv & appr

> Isaac & his wife Milly, Jackson, Madison, Edward, Amanda, Jinny, Juliet, Ellen, Sally, Frances, Nancy, John, Thomas, William

Johnathan WATERS .... pg 461, 13 June 1842, inv & appr

> women Katy, Henrietta, Maria, Sarah, boys Solomon, Frank, Albert, Warner, girls Eloisa, Julianna, child Elizabeth

Henry BYWATER .... pg 471, 13 Sept 1839, inv & appr

> Lewis age 40, Levi 25, Daphney 27, Lucy Ann 12, Harriet 8, Caroline 5, Elizabeth 3, Charles 10 months old

Ann WATERS .... pg 473, 20 Aug 1842, dower

> Caty, Solomon, Maria, Henrietta, Sarah, Frank, Warren, Elvira, Elizabeth, Albert, Julianna

WILL BOOK B

1842-1849

John CROPP.. pg 18, 29 Dec 1841, inv & appr

    Frank age 60, Lewis 40, Milly 37, Eloya 36, Bennett 23, Lucy 18, Susan 15, Mary 13, Walker 14, Strother 11, boy ___, boy Henry, girls Betsy Ann, Felicia, boy Resin, girl Hester, boy Welford, girl Henny

Ann PULLER... pg 23, 27 Dec 1839, acct of sales

    man Garret to Richard T. RISEY; man Thomas to William K. ALMOND; man Robert to Mann ALMOND; woman Isabella to James PARR; woman Phillis to William W. CARTER

Rhoda HAYNIE..................... pg 24, 4 Jan 1838 – 10 Dec 1842, adm acct

    Emanuel hired

Sarah E., Richard A., George Anna, Lucretia A. & Thadeus HAYNIE......
.... pg 26, 1841 - 1842, gdn acct

    2 women & 3 children, man Emanuel, woman Fanny, girls Lucinda, Rosetta

Anthony HAYNIE.................... pg 26, 6 Nov 1841 – 7 Jan 1843, adm acct

    girls Lucinda, Rosetta, Summerville, Eliza, Maria sold

George CHEEK... pg 31, 21 Dec 1842, will

    boy Charles to son Lawson CHEEK; girl Amy to daughter Isabella CHEEK; woman to daughter Dicy CHEEK; none of negroes to be sold; Minor, Phil to son Elijah CHEEK; old Jacob, old Winney, old Phillis to have choice of legatees; negro families not to be divided

Elijah SETTLE.................................pg 33, 17 Dec 1842, inv & appr

> Taliafero age 33, Nelson 31, Tom 29, Sam 28, Alfred 26, Solomon 24, Bill 25, Lewis 19, Thornton 17, Silvy 23 & children Mary Ann 4 & Frank 9 months; Haney 20 & children Lucy Ann 3 & John 1; Milly 13, Mary 12, Jane 9, Jude 53

Robert SLAUGHTER........................pg 36, 12 Nov 1841, inv & appr

> boy Jack, girls Mary, Eve, boy Henry

George CHEEK................................pg 38, 21 Jan 1843, inv & appr

> Bob, Adam, Thornton, Albert, Reuben, Henry, Strother, Eve, Susan & 2 children Tom & Catherine, Charity & 2 children Alcinda & Henny, Hannah & 2 children Miner & George, Maria & 2 children Bob & Harry, Jim, Mary, Ellen, Elisa, Polly, Caroline, Tilda, Emily & child Fanny, Ann, Henrietta, Eveline, Champ, Jim; Miner, Phil E. CHEEK has had; boy Charles to L. CHEEK; girl Amy to Isabella CHEEK

Robert SLAUGHTER....................pg 41, 24 – 26 Nov 1842, acct of sales

> girl Mary to Mason BROWNING; girl Eve to John S. BUCKNER; boy Henry to George W. PENDLETON; boy Jack to William JOHNSON Jr.

Michael NICOL.....................pg 48, 25 Oct 1840 – 3 Jan 1843, adm acct

> Thornton (free boy)

William E. JONES .... pg 52, 11 Mar 1843, settlement

> ...to equalize the division of the slaves...

William E. JONES .... pg 54, 31 Mar 1838 – 20 Jan 1843, adm acct

> cost of suit for division of slaves; Elizabeth JONES widow, Charles E. JONES, George W. JONES, Mary V. JONES, Lucy M. JONES, Sarah E. JONES, Lawson B. JONES

William E. JONES. .... pg 60, 1 Jan 1836 – 31 Dec 1842, list of slaves

 Samuel 45, Meredith 21, Shubael 11, Lewis 8, Washington 8, Celia 52, Haner 20 & child, Hannah 17, Eliza 15, Harriet 12, Adaline 12, Mary 6, Kitty 9

Sarah E. JONES & others.....pg 60, 31 Dec 1836 – 31 Dec 1842, gdn acct & others: Sarah Elizabeth JONES, Mary Virginia JONES, George William JONES, Charles Eastham JONES, Lucy Margaret JONES, & Lawson Byrd JONES; hire of slaves

JONES et al ....pg 64, 13 Mar 18_3, commissioner's acct

 William E. JONES died summer or fall of 1835; slaves in possession of Elizabeth JONES widow, divided 23 Dec 1842; 7 negroes under age 8 in 1836 & 7; 5 under age 8 in 1838, 4 under age 8 in 1839 & 40; 3 in 1841; 2 in 1842

Benjamin BASYE .... pg 68, 1 May 1843, adm acct

 boy, girl Ellen sold

William DEATHERAGE .... pg 71, 5 Apr 1843, inv & appr

 Harry 57, George 36, Henry 32, Tom 28, Davy 26, Peter 23, Nelson 23, Lewis 16, Richard 15, Jack 15, Alfred 15, Charles 12, Joseph 8, Armistead 3, Marshall 9 mo, Elizabeth 7, Nancy 5, Clary 24 (children of Clary), Sarah 18, Drusilla 4, Minor 2, Susan infant (children of Sarah), Levina 43, Sophia 18, Amanda 14, Rosaline 11 Mary 10, Ellen 7

Thomas SPINDLE .... pg 93, 17 Apr 1843, will

 Daniel, Jemima, George & Agga his wife with her 2 children Mary & Emily (little George being the property of William A. SPINDLE), Peter & Milly his wife, Melinda, Nelson, Walker, Thompson, Jennette & child to wife Elizabeth; after death of my wife George & his wife Agga with their youngest child to Eveline; Margaret to daughter Emily M.A. BOWEN; residue of negroes to be divided among children Evelina S., John P., Harriet C., William A., Elisa V., Adaline A., Thomas G., Robert H., & granddaughter Betty W. CARSON; Judy, Edy to son John P. SPINDLE; Gayden & child, Caroline Getty, Lucinda to daughter Harriet C. THROOP; boy Landford to son William A. SPINDLE; Martha & child to Evelina; Matilda to Eliza; Mary to Adaline

Mary C. LATHAM late AMISS..
....pg 100, 18 Apr 1833 – 1 July 1837, gdn acct
negro money

Mary C. LATHAM late AMISS..
.... pg 102, 24 May 1838 – 1 Nov 1843, gdn acct

negroes belonging to Philip N. AMISS sold

John H. WOOD... pg 106, 19 Jan 1844, inv & appr

men Edmund, Isaac, woman Jemima, girls Mariah, Mary, boy Henry, girl Emily, man Cato

Thomas Richard BYWATER...
....pg 114, 31 Dec 1840 – 31 Dec 1842, gdn acct
negroes hired

Robert H. BYWATER........pg 116, 31 Dec 1840 – 31 Dec 1842, gdn acct
negroes hired

Henry MENEFEE .... pg 120, 15 Mar 1844, inv & appr

boys Walker, Lewis, Robin, Charles, Gilbert, George, Albert, Armistead, James, girl Fanny, boy Jerry, girl Rachel, man Will, woman Hannah, man Bill, Mary & child, girl Eliza, Jacob, woman Lizzy

Henry MENEFEE ....pg 124, 28 & 29 Mar 1844, acct of sales

boy Walker to Slaughter __ry; boy Lewis, Hannah & child, man Bill to Willis BROWNING; boys Robin, Charles, Mary & child, girl Eliza to James A. BROWNING; boy Jacob to Thomas CARPENTER; boy Albert to Arthur NELSON; boy Gilbert to Alexander F. MENEFEE; boy George to Walt OBANNON; girl Fanny to Elisha PAR_LOW; boys Armistead, James to William YAGER; girl Rachel to O.P. SMITH; old man Bill to J.B. GORE

John CROPP.. pg 130, 22 Jan 1844, adm acct

negro to William BYWATER; Lucy hired; girl to David RITENOUR

Daniel UPDIKE... pg 142, 17 Apr 1844, inv & appr

George age 21, Harper 17

William BROWN............................... pg 151, 23 Jan 1844, inv & appr

Thomas, Henry, Mary & child Harriet, Sarah, Catherine, Winney & 3 children Frank, Eliza, & Rachel, Leah, Washington Kizziah

William A. LANE................................pg 153, 17 Nov 1842, inv & appr

Sally age 45 & child Lavinia, Jack 28, French 26, George 24, Enoch 19, Edward 17, Woodson 15, Jane 13, Frank 10, Charles Robert 8, Christopher 6, Emily 22 & child Letty, Nancy 39 & child Bundy, Austin 6, Winney 40 & children Amanda & Nelly, Henry 20, Bill 18, Sam 16, Adaline 14, Malvina 10, Sarah Catherine 8, Horace 5, Mima 26 & children Joe, Lucy, & Milly, Charlotte 32 & children Matilda 13, Anaky, Harriet, Betsy & Alcinda, Warrenton 11, Ann Maria 9, Charity 35 & children Susan & Patsy, Daniel 16, Jones 14, Caroline 10, Clara 37 & children Somerville, Turner, & Alice, Marshall 19, Fanny 13, Joe Lewis 11, Aaron 9, Caroline 39 & child Cornelia, George Washington 19, Reuben 16, Ben 12, Ned 10, Margaret 6, Louisa 40 & children Lizzy & Ellick, Madison 19, Manuel 17, E__ 15, Lewis 10, Sam 6, Polly 25 & children Phillis, Isabella, & Lydia, Judy 45, Jim 15, Manuel 10, Sam 50, Bob 40, Sawney 40, Arch 29, Lewis 15, Mark 12; the following will belong to the estate at the death of Mrs. Getty SMITHER: Jane 17, Ann 15, Kitty 13, Tom 20

Elizabeth SPILLER .... pg 169, 1 Jan 1843, will

   all negroes to daughter Tamar SPILLER

Joshua HOPPER .... pg 170, 31 May 1844, will

   slaves to be disposed of and to choose their masters...& not sold to foreign traders

Elizabeth SPILLER .... pg 174, 10 Aug 1844, inv & appr

   women Nancy, Charlotte, Sephrona, boys Jim, Isaac, Rousey, Bailey, Wesley, Tom, Jones, girl Eliza, boy Jarrott

James GREEN .... pg 177, 18 Jan 1841, codicil

   boy Frederick to great granddaughter Elizabeth Lane SCOTT & if she does not reach the age of 21 to my grandson John G. LANE in trust for M. Frances SCOTT & her heirs

James GREEN .... pg 177, 27 May 1843, codicil

   revoke gift of Frederick to great granddaughter Elizabeth Lane SCOTT and give him his freedom

John D. BROWNING .... pg 183, 11 Oct 1844, will

   slaves from first wife & property received by both marriages up to this date...wishing to make all my children by both wives equal out of the whole estate...1/3 to wife Cassandra BROWNING & on her death to be equally divided among all children including my first set & my last set

Elijah SETTLE .... pg 186, 29 Dec 1842, list of sales

   man Alfred to Hannah BANNON; hired out: Nelson, Milly, Tom, Mary, Alfred, Sam, Solomon, Lewis, Thornton, Bill, Juda, Jane, Hanney & children Lucy Ann & John, Taliafero, Silvey & children left ot attend to widow

Robert Henry BYWATER ....
....pg 196, 31 Dec 1843 – Dec 1844, gdn acct

   boy Charles, girl Lucy, Caroline

Thomas Richard BYWATER ....
....pg 197, 31 Dec 1843 – Dec 1844, gdn acct

   Levi, Harriet

Joshua HOPPER Sr. ....pg 198, 25 Aug 1844, inv & appr

   Celia, Angelina, Anthony, French

Joshua HOPPER Sr. ....pg 199, 23 Aug 1844, acct of sales

   man Anthony to Lewis D. MASSIE; Celia & her child Angelina to James POWERS; boy French to John HOPPER

John D. BROWNING .... pg 204, Jan 1845, inv & appr

   Strother, Jarred, Addison, James, Peter, Daniel, Isham, Lewis, Isaac, Ned, Temple, French, Burrell, Spencer, Delsy & child, Aggy, Ellen, Rose, Clary, Martha, Sarah Virginia

John D. BROWNING .... pg 208, 1 Mar 1845, estate div

   Strother age 40 or 45, Jarred 40 or 45, Addison 33, James 28, Peter 25, Daniel 19, Isham 17, Lewis 16, Isaac 14, Ned 9, Temple 6, French 4, Burrell 3, Spencer, Delsy 38 & child Charlotte, Aggy 36 & child not named, Ellen 12, Rose 30, Clary, 6 Martha 5, Sarah Virginia 2

   Strother, Jarred, Aggy & child, Ellen, Lewis, Spencer, French to dower; Delsey & child, Ned to Margaret BROWNING; Peter, Temple to M__ BROWNING; Addison, Clary to E.S. BROWNING; James, Martha to Henrietta BROWNING; Daniel, Sarah Virginia to G.J. BROWNING; Isham, Burrell to Frances L. BROWNING; Isaac, Rose to John S. BROWNING

Daniel UPDIKE Sr. .... pg 225, 8 Aug 1844, acct of sales
> man George to Hannah UPDIKE; man Anthony to Lafayette S. MENEFEE

Burr WOODWELL .... pg 229, 26 Apr 1845, inv & appr
> Thornton Lewis, Milly, Susan, Roxaline, Louisa, Philip, Minor, George

William B. BROOKE .... pg 237, 1845, inv & appr
> man Daniel, girl Leah, boys Jim, Thornton

Tabitha MENEFEE .... pg 243, 11 Sept 1845, inv & appr
> man George, woman Letty, Ellen & 2 children

Tabitha MENEFEE .... pg 245, 12 Sept 1845, acct of sales
> Ellen & 2 children to Elijah AMISS; man George, woman Letty to James A. MENEFEE

George W. JONES .... pg 252, 31 Dec 1843 – 14 Aug 1844, gdn acct
> girl hired

Charles E. JONES .... pg 252, 31 Dec 1843 – 14 Aug 1844, gdn acct
> man Meredith hired

Lucy Margaret JONES ...... pg 252, 31 Dec 1843 – 14 Aug 1844, gdn acct
> boy hired

Lawson Bird JONES .... pg 254, 31 Dec 1843 – 14 Aug 1844, gdn acct
> negroes hired

Robert HISLE .... pg 254, 18 Oct 1845, estate div
> Lydia, Phil, Manuel, Ned, Tom, Pompey, Jack, Frank, Joshua,

Dennis, Alfred, Stuart, Jim, Eveline & child, Fanny & children Fanny & William, Betsy & child Francis, Mary & child Mary Ann, Dolly, Susan, Henrietta, Champ Broadus, Howard, Jane, Barbara, Charlotte, Ellen, Amanda, Felicia, Eliza, Lucretia, Celia

girl Jane to Samuel HISLE; girl Barbara, Jack, Lydia to Champ HISLE; boy Howard, girl Dolly, Stuart, Fanny & 2 children to John P. HISLE, man Pompey, girl Celia, Emanuel, Betsy & child to Agnes HISLE; man Frank, girl Lucretia, Joshua, Mary & child, Ellen to Thomas HISLE; Tom, Felicia to George HISLE; Phillis, Charles, Henrietta to Francis TANCIL; Ned, Eveline & child, Amanda to Sam HISLE; Dennis, Alfred, Jane to Jesse HISLE

William BROWN .... pg 268, 1 Jan 1844 – 22 Oct 1845, exec acct

Harry, 2 negroes

Bryant OBANNON .... pg 269, 23 Oct 1841, will

women Lucinda, Ann & their increase in possession of John & Nancy BRADY to be brought to the estate to be included in the division among all my children: John M. OBANNON, Walter OBANNON, Joseph OBANNON, Sarah OBANNON, Mary OBANNON, James OBANNON, Jane OBANNON, Charles Bryant OBANNON, Eliza OBANNON, & Lucy OBANNON

Elizabeth BERKLEY .... pg 272, 7 Feb 1843, will

girl Dolly to Susan F. BERKLEY

Edwin A. CROPP .... pg 280, 1842 - 1845, gdn acct

division of negroes; Lucy, Lewis, Presley, Milly, girl, Felicia

Robert HISLE .... pg 295, 15 Jan 1845 - 1 Apr 1845, adm acct

negro hire

Elizabeth A.W. CARSON .... pg 301, 14 Sept 1846, inv & appr

boy Howard, girl Betsy, boy Jones, Jenetta & child Daniel

Benjamin BLACKWELL................................pg 303, 23 July 1846, will

    Esther 8 to daughter Katharine A. SAUNDERS; Fanny to daughter Elizabeth ROBINSON

Elizabeth A.W. CARSON..........pg 304, 28 May – 31 Dec 1845, gdn acct

    Howard, Jenetta

James GREEN....................pg 306, 10 Dec 1844 – 5 Nov 1846, exec acct

    Frederick sold

Bryant OBANNON............................. pg 335, 23 Jan 1846, inv & appr

    men Thomas, Samuel, Robert, Benjamin, James, Charles, Abraham, women Matilda, Terry, Maria, Lib, Harriet, Ellen, Catherine, girl Matilda, boys Henry, Marshall, Judson, Burley

Eliza V. SPINDLE .... pg 346, 28 Dec 1846, inv & appr

    man Nelson, woman Matilda, boys Bailer, John, woman Jemima

Benjamin BLACKWELL.......................pg 350, 16 Nov 1846, inv & appr

    men Littleton, Daniel, girls Emily, Violet, Delila & child

Ezekiel BRANDOM ....pg 351, 26 Nov 1d843, will

    slaves to be sold after death of wife Sarah Ann

Robert HUDSON ....pg 355, 1846, will

    choice of 5 negroes to wife Elizabeth HUDSON; remainder to be divided among children: Joshua HUDSON, Armistead HUDSON, Alfred HUDSON, John W. HUDSON, Susan HUDSON, Jale RUDASELLA, & Margaret DORSEY

Lewis MOORE......................... pg 359, 19 Jan 1847, inv & appr

    except the slaves

Lewis MOORE................................pg 360, 21 Jan 1847, acct of sales

    man William to Alfina DEARING

David RITENOUR.............................pg 366, 18 May 1846, inv & appr

    man Washington, girl Mary

William B. BROOKE..........................pg 367, 27 Oct 1845, estate div

    man Daniel, girl Leah, boys Thornton, Jim
    girl Leah to Hannah S. BROOKE; boys Thornton, Jim to William H. ROBERTS in right of his wife; man Daniel to Gidean H. BOWEN in right of his wife

Robert HUDSON..............................pg 374, 17 Mar 1847, inv & appr

    man Gilbert, boys Henry, Ben, woman Winney, girl Ellen left to his wife Elizabeth HUDSON

Robert HUDSON..............................pg 375, 17 Mar 1847, inv & appr

    old men James, Caleb, old woman Charlotte, Juda & 2 children, Clara & 2 children Aaron & Hannah, boy Peter, man Charles, girls Hester, Ann, Martha

Thomas H. FISHER...........................pg 377, 30 July 1846, inv & appr

    woman Juliet, man Alfred

Burwell K. WOOD............pg 383, 18 Apr 1845 – 19 Feb 1847, exec acct

    negroes hired

Ezekiel BRANDOM ....pg 385, 16 Mar 1847, inv & appr

    boy John, old woman Charlotte, Jane & her child Mary Ann, boy Bob, old man Billy

Ezekiel BRANDOM ....pg 388, 19 & 20 Mar 1847, acct of sales
   boy John to James OBANNON; boy Bob to Andrew R. BARBEE; old man Billy, old woman Charlotte to William WALDEN; Jane & her child Mary Ann to Albert C. WOODARD

William WATERS .... pg 398, 26 June 1847, inv & appr
   old woman Aggy

Moses GREEN .... pg 401, 6 July 1847, inv & appr
   old woman Fanny

Margaret DUNCAN ....pg 407, 10 Aug 1845 – 23 June 1847, adm acct
   negroes to E. CHEEK

William WATERS ....pg 411, 19 July 1847, acct of sales
   woman to C.T. WATERS

Robert JONES... pg 414, 4 June 1847, inv & appr
   woman Mary, men Jaseh, Carter, boy Jackson

Tabitha MENEFEE ....pg 417, 12 Sept 1845 - 7 Jan 1848, adm acct
   Sally to T.S. MENEFEE

William BROWN...............pg 422, 22 Oct 1845 - 23 Mar 1847, exec acct
   man Harry

Robert H. BYWATER ....pg 424, 1 Jan 1845 – 31 Dec 1847, gdn acct
   boy Charles, Caroline, Lucy Ann

Thomas R. BYWATER..........pg 426, 1 Jan 1845 – 31 Dec 1847, gdn acct
   Lewis, Harriet, Levi

Cornelius HUFF ....pg 434, 16 Mar 1848, inv & appr

> boy George

George James GREEN ....pg 435, 2 Mar 1848, inv & appr

> Jesse age 50, Milly 40, Mary 22, Susan 27, Jack 23, Edward 19, Daniel 6

Agnes SETTLE .... pg 436, 31 Dec 1843 – 8 May 1848, comm acct

> man Toliver, girl Mary, boy Bill

Zephaniah TURNER ....pg 449, 8 Oct 1844, will

> girl Sarah Martha daughter of little Maria to granddaughter Jane Maria TURNER; Harriet daughter of Pat to granddaughter Susan TURNER; girl to be selected for granddaughter Anna TURNER; boy Elzy son of little Maria to grandson Lewis TURNER; boy Henry to grandson John Robert TURNER; in selling slaves husbands & wives to be together

Thomas WALDEN ....pg 459, 18 July 1848, inv & appr

> man Davy, Priscilla age 80, Facey & children Jeffry, Cora, Mary, Charlotte, Elizabeth, Priscilla, & Alcinda

Eliza V. SPINDLE .... pg 461, 8 June 1846 – 7 Sept 1848, adm acct

> Nelson; negro hire; div of negroes

Lewis MOORE ....pg 469, 3 Jan 1847 – 1 Sept 1848, exec acct

> boy Will

Joshua HOPPER ....pg 473, 9 Nov 1846 – 1 July 1848, exec acct

> Celia & child to James L. POWERS; French to Charles H. FLINN: Anthony to Lewis D. MASSIE

.... pg 475, acct of advancements

> boy Robert, girl Ann, Hene & son Andreas, Elizabeth to John

29

HOPPER; girl Amanda, boy William, girl Betsy, boy Hanson, girl Miriam to Joshua HOPPER: girl Maria, Eliza, Jane, Jennifer to Miriam AMISS

Lucy WALDEN .... pg 483, 31 Aug 1848, will

Facey & her 7 children Mary, Charlotte, Elizabeth, Priscilla, Alcinda, Jeffry, & Cora, old man Davy, old woman Priscilla to son Carnot M. WALDEN; 11 + negroes in Missouri in possession of son William M. WALDEN to be sold

Mary FISHER .... pg 486, 28 Dec 1848, div of slaves

Moses, Joanna, Harriet, Daniel, Emily & child, Roxaline, Ned, Louisa, Lewis

Moses, Harriet, Daniel, Roxaline to Robert EASTHAM; Joanna, Emily & child, Ned, Louisa, Lewis to Lucy FISHER guardian of the children of Thomas H. FISHER dc'd

John T. ROYSTON .... pg 488, 31 Dec 1847, inv & appr

Frances age 30, Mary 2 1/2, Frank 4, William 6, Thomas 8

Lucy WALDEN .... pg 489, 13 Jan 1849, inv & appr

Facey & infant child Sally & children Mary, Charlotte, Patsy, Priscilla, Alcinda, Jeffry, & Cora, old woman Priscilla, David 55

John D. BROWNING .... pg 495, 19 Jan 1849, commissoner's report

a negro
.... pg 496, 10 May 1847 – 31 Dec 1848, exec acct
Daniel

John CORDER .... pg 499, 17 June 1835, will

man Frank, woman Beck to wife Hannah CORDER; remainder of slaves to be divided among my children Sarah HANDSUCKER, Vincent CORDER, Elizabeth COWGILL, the children of son Elisha

CORDER dec'd, Martha CORDER, Nathan CORDER, John CORDER Jr., Polly JACKSON, & Elias CORDER; boy Philip to the children of son Elijah CORDER

Silas FRISTOE .... pg 503, 30 Aug 1847, inv & appr

girl Ellen, Matilda & her 2 children

John UPDIKE .... pg 505, 11 May 1848, inv & appr

Warner age 11, girl Julian 10, George 7, boy Albert, girl Martha, boy William

Nicolas BROWN .... pg 507, 13 Feb 1849, inv & appr

Dicy & 2 youngest children Jane & Ann, boy Silas, girls Malinda, Madlum, boys French, John

Susan DUNCAN .... pg 528, 26 May 1849, inv & appr

woman Nancy, Mary & child, boy Henry

Ann COXE .... pg 530, 14 Jan 1848, inv & appr

Beverly age 45, Benjamin 25, Eli 28, George 22, Mark 16, Turner 15, Henry 8, Elvira 10, Mary 9, John 6, Hansborough 6, Davy 3, Eveline 30 & child, Maria, 48, Jaqueline 19

.... pg 536, 16 Feb 1848, acct of sales

man George to Lewis D. MASSIE; man Ben, Evelina & child, girl Mary, boys John, Davy to James LETT; boy Mark Anthony to John LETT Sr., boy Turner to L.H. KNIGHT; man Eli to John GIVENS; man Beverly to James & John LETT; woman Jaqueline to Benjamin F. HEINSEY; woman Marge & boy to J. BARTON; girl Elvira to J.M. OBANNON; boy Henry to B. CARVER

Silas FRISTOE .... pg 547, 26 Aug 1847 – 1 Oct 1849, adm acct

woman Matilda to S.H. KNIGHT

WILL BOOK C

1849-1855

William P. BROWN..................................pg 1, 8 Nov 1849, will

woman Adelaide, Furlong, Edmund, Russel to wife Mary A. BROWN; Milly & her child; boy Thornton to son Thomas W. BROWN; William, Howard, Eliza & her child to son James M. BROWN; Harry, Ann, Sarah, Caroline, Catherine, Lewis, to son F.C. Newton BROWN; Stephen, Mary, Susan, Ocean, Henry to daughter Willie E. BROWN; old Tom to F.C. Newton BROWN to be free if he wishes; Thomton to be retained by F.C. Newton BROWN

William P. BROWN.................................. pg 4, 21 Dec 1849, inv & appr

free negroes who were bound to the dc'd in his lifetime: George born 27 July 1833, Stepney b 1 Apr 1835, Pender b 15 Jan 1837, Maria b 25 Aug 1838, Harriet b 15 Mar 1840, Henrietta b 26 Feb 1842; the men to serve until age 21, the women age 18

John UPDIKE.....................................pg 7, 25 May 1848, list of sales

boy George, child Martha to Mrs. Ury UPDIKE; boy Warner to Francis M. PERRY, girl Julia to William PERRY; boy Albert to David McKAY

Nicholas BROWNING.........pg 9, 27 Sept 1847 – 1 Feb 1849, comm acct

French, Billy, woman, negro

Joseph FRISTOE.............................. pg 16, 12 Apr 1850, inv & appr

Albert, Henry

Martin CLIZER...........................pg 18, 23 Oct 1849, inv & appr

Mary & child 5 months old. Frank age 7, Henry 6, Malinda 4

Jacob REAGEN.. pg 27, 27 Dec 1849, inv & appr

old woman Winney , girl Dulceny, boy Peter, old man Billy

Jacob REAGEN..pg 31, 28 Dec 1849, list of sales

old man Billy, old woman Winney , boy Peter to Mary REAGEN; girl Dulceny to John A. REAGEN

Andrew GAUNT.. pg 45, 8 May 1850, will

man Thornton to son Isaiah GAUNT; woman Polly to daughter Ellen SWINDLER; woman Theodosia to daughter Sarah CORBIN; boy Edward to son Daniel GAUNT; boy George to son William GAUNT; remaining negroes except woman Alcinda & her children & girl China to be evenly divided between children Alpheus GAUNT, Daniel GAUNT, William GAUNT, Isaiah GAUNT, Elizabeth GROVES, Ellen SWINDLER, & Sarah CORBIN; woman Alcinda - child to son William GAUNT in trust for daughter Nancy TURLEY; girl China to son William GAUNT in trust for daughter Rebecca CORBIN

Thomas BYWATERS............pg 48, 20 Jan 1848 – 31 Dec 1849, gdn acct

Harriet & new born child; Levi; Harriet's child died; Lewis; Harriet with a young child

Robert H. BYWATERS.........pg 50, 20 Jan 1848 – 31 Dec 1849, gdn acct

Lucy Ann, Caroline

James George GREEN........pg 53, 21 Sept 1847 – 21 Apr 1850, exec acct

Susan, Jesse, Milly, Isaac, Edward, Jack

Mary SLOAN.. pg 57, 3 June 1847, will

woman Elmira to be set free; Sarah, Georgianna, Charles, Cassey to friend John S. HUGHES

Zadock SEDWICK................................pg 59, 8 Feb 1850, will

½ the value of woman Amanda, girl Mary to son William H. SEDWICK after death of my wife Elizabeth SEDWICK; girl Alcinda, ¼ of the value of ½ of woman Amanda, ¼ part of the value of Amanda's children to son James B. SEDWICK after death of my wife; 1 negro share to the children of dec'd daughter Peggy HARRINGTON: George W. HARRINGTON, Susan E. HARRINGTON, & Zadock HERRINGTON to be divided equally; Ruth & her 2 sons Joe & Tom, ¼ of the value of ¼ the value of Amanda & her children to son James B. SEDWICK; James B. SEDWICK to apply same annually to Elvira SEDWICK & children of son Benjamin SEDWICK; ½ the value of Amanda & ¼ the value of her children to daughter Dolly COWGILL; ¼ the value of ½ of woman Amanda & ½ the value of her children to granddaughter Susan E. HARRINGTON

Silas FRISTOE................................pg 92, 1 Sept 1847, list of sales

22 Sept 1848: woman Matilda to L.H. KNIGHT;

9 Sept 1850: girl Ellen to Goldam negro trader

Henry SWINDLER................................ pg 100, 27 Apr 1850, inv & appr

boy Daniel

Silas FRISTOE.................. pg 103, 21 Nov 1849 – 1 July 1850, adm acct

Ellen

Sarah MAJORS................................pg 106, 2 Aug 1842, will

boy Richard to daughter Jamima Jane the wife of Isaac WILSON; woman Emily to daughter Frances

William P. BROWN............................ pg 108, 24 Dec 1849, list of sales

boy George to Henry REAGEN; boy Stephney to James MADDOX; girl Pender to Henry C. BARBEE; girl Mariah to Eastham JORDAN; girl Harriet to B.W. MYERS; girl Henrietta to John T. BALL

Catherine WITHERS alias HILLARY ....
....pg 112, 19 Feb 1849, inv & appr

    Willis, Jack, Edmond, Aaron, Prince, Benjamin, Kate & child Henry, Daniel, Lige, Wagonam, Hannah, Tamey alias Dick, Ann, Lucy & child Clary

Peter DEAL ....pg 118, 18 Nov 1850, will

    slaves to be divided in 6 equal parts; 1 lot to include girl Frances to James DEAL; 1 lot to include girl Sarah to daughter Malinda F. SEDWICK & her husband George W. SEDWICK; 1 lot to include Ann & her child to executors Allen L. DEAL & George W. SEDWICK in trust for daughter Cassandra McQUEEN wife of Boswell McQUEEN; 1 lot to said executors in trust for son Robert DEAL; 1 lot to daughter Margaret Ann DEAL; 1 lot to son Allen L. DEAL

Peter DEAL .... pg 130, 27 Dec 1850, div of slaves

    Charles, Matt, John, George, Ann & child Elvira, Harriet & child Jane, Bethana & child Lucy, Nancy & child Alice, Maria, Frances, Sarah, little Sarah, Dallas, Cora, Hammet, Ellen, Mary, Amanda, Margaret, Henry

    Sarah, Hammet, Maria, Margaret to George W. SEDWICK; Matt, Henry, Nancy & child Alice to Allen L. DEAL; Frances, Bethana & child Lucy, little Sarah, Dallas to James DEAL; George, Ellen, Mary to George W. SEDWICK & Allen L. DEAL in trust for Robert DEAL; John, Harriet & child Jane, Amanda to Margaret DEAL; Ann & child Elvira, Charles, Cora to George W. SEDWICK & Allen L. DEAL in trust for Cassandra McQUEEN

Henry SWINDLER .... pg 132, 27 Apr 1850, acct of sales

    boy Daniel to J. McLATHAM

William SMITH .... pg 141, 13 Dec 1850, inv & appr

    man Lewis, boy Uriah, girls Matilda, Bet, Ann

William SMITH................................ pg 142, 16 Dec 1850, list of sales

    man Lewis to John MILLER; woman Matilda, girl Betty to Thomas GOLDING; boy Uriah girl Ann to H.T. SPARKS

Peter DEAL .... pg 145, 26 Dec 1850, inv & appr

    men Madison, Charles, George, John, woman Maria, Ann & child, Harriet & child, girl Ellen, Frances, Amanda, Margaret, boy Hammet, Henry, Dallas, Cora, big Sarah, little Sarah, Bethana & child, Nancy & child

Susannah JETT................................ pg 155, 30 Dec 1850, inv & appr

    Lewis age 25, Henderson 22, Jackson 20, Bradford 18, Mela & 2 children Dallas & Thomas, Lucy & 2 children Susan & James, Eliza 14, Martha 14, Somerfield 11, Maria 9, Wesley 9

William P. BROWN........................... pg 168, 3 Dec 1850, inv & appr

    Furlong age 25, Edward 21, Thornton 16, Lewis 12, Milly 18 & child, Russell 23, Adelaide 18 & child, Henry

John CORDER .... pg 169, 23 May 1849, inv & appr

    old man Ralph & Rebecca his wife, old man Frank, Mary & child Mary Jane, young man Strother, boys Wesley, Allen, girl Martha, boy William, girls Evelina, Nancy

John CORDER .... pg 170, 1 Aug 1849, list of sales

    Mary & child to Elias CORDER; Strother, Wesley to John CORDER; Allen to Daniel JACKSON; Martha to Nathan CORDER; Frank, William to Isham CORDER; Evelina to Bueler CORDER; Nancy to Elias CORDER; Ralph & Becky to Elias CORDER & F.M. JEFFRIES

Elizabeth SEDWICK........................pg 174, 21 Feb 1851, inv & appr

    woman Amanda, girl Delia, boys Jack, George

Elizabeth SEDWICK..............................pg 175, 21 Feb 1851, list of sales

   woman Amanda, child, boy Dick to Alfred COWGILL; girl Delia to James COWGILL

Andrew GAUNT................................pg 179, 6 Sept 1850, div of slaves

   Hannah, Richard, Dianna, Sarah, Agga, Maria, Arthur, Charles, Angelina, John, Frank, Rosella, Woodson, Mildred, Delia, William

   Lot 1: Hannah, Richard; Lot 2: Dianna, Sarah, Agga; Lot 3: Maria, Arthur; Lot 4: Charles; Lot 5: Angelina, John; Lot 6: Frank; Lot 7: Rosella, Woodson; Lot 8: Mildred; Lot 9: Delia, William

   Lot 1 to William GAUNT trustee of Nancy TURLEY; Lot 2 to Isaiah GAUNT; Lot 3 to Daniel GAUNT; Lot 4 to William GAUNT trustee of Rebecca CORBIN; Lot 5 to Sarah CORBIN; Lot 6 to Alpheus GAUNT; Lot 7 to Elizabeth GROVES; Lot 8 to William GAUNT; Lot 9 to Ellen SWINDLER

George BOWYER.................................pg 181, 16 Aug 1851, inv & appr

   woman & child

John HOPPER.................................... pg 189, 21 June 1851, inv & appr

   man Bob, woman Henny, Ann & child, girl Betsy, boys Smith, George

John HOPPER..pg 191, 15 Aug 1851, list of sales

   boy George, Ann & child Lewis, boy Smith to Richard H. TIMBERLAKE

Dicy TAPP .... pg 193, 9 June 1851, inv & appr

   Jacly, Hannah, Ann, Mary & child, Celia & child, Ellen, Somerville, Martha, Lucinda, Louisa, Henry

Frances BURGESS .... pg 195, May 1847, will

   Henry, Delia & all her children, Sally to daughter Catherine BURGESS

....pg 198, Sept 1851, codicil

woman Melinda to daughters Ann CAMP & Catherine BURGESS

Frances BURGESS ....pg 213, 19 Nov 1851, inv & appr

boys Arthur, Middleton, girls Ellen, Phoebe, Mary & child, girls Mima, Charlotte, Alcey & child, girl Eliza, boy Bob, man Edmund, child Melinda, child Sally, women Maria, Caroline, Lucy, Melinda, girl Jinny, boy Billy, girl Jane, boy Elias, man Henry, woman Sally,

Elijah AMISS ....pg 221, 7, 8, 11 Feb 1852, inv & appr

men Washington, Jim, boy Nelson, old woman Daphney, man Armistead, woman & child Emily & Ema_e, girls Lucy, Esther, boys Morton, Henry, Peter, girl Somerville, men Randall, Bartlett, woman Evelina, Maria & child Robert, boy French, Hester Ann & child William, girls Jane, Ann, boy Horace, woman Rose, girl Eve, boy Marcus, Susan & child Rose, girl Martha, woman Jamima, girl Dicey boys Orange, Caesar, girl Belle, man Joe, girl Minerva, old man Ben ....pg 225, inv of bonds

Edith, Minerva

Elijah AMISS ....pg 226, 11, 12 Feb 1852, list of sales

man Washington to H.G. JONES; man James to Walter OBANNON; man Joe to W.H. GAINES; man Randall to George FICKLIN; men Bartlett, Armistead, boy Morton, Maria & child, woman Eveline, girl Esther, Hester Ann & 4 children, Susan & 2 children, Emily & 3 children, Maria, Orange, Daphney to Ann E. AMISS; boys French, Carson to Peter JOHNSON; boy Nelson to John W. CARMEN; woman Rose to J.A. MENEFEE; Jinnie to W.S. ALCOCK; girl Somerville to Joseph B_AGE; girl Eve to R.C. LATHAM; girl Lucy to Richard THORNHILL; girl Dicy to A.F. GREEN; Belle to H.W. AMISS; Washington, Jim sold; Minerva hired to W.H. BURKE; old Ben died 15 Feb

Theoderick HUFF .... pg 233, 23 Feb 1852, list of sales

    girl to James M. OBANNON

William H. SEDWICK .... pg 234, 12 Apr 1852, inv & appr

    girl Mary

Mary W. DEATHERAGE .... pg 241, 10 May 1852, div of slaves

    Jack, Betsy, Nancy, Armistead, Marshall, Clary, Mary, Chancello, Vina, Mary

    Jack to Robert DEATHERAGE; Betsy to James MOORE & Maria his wife; Nancy to John DEATHERAGE; Armistead to Philip DEATHERAGE; Clary to Elizabeth FANT late DEATHERAGE; Mary to George DEATHERAGE; Chancello, Vina to William A. DEATHERAGE

Susan DUNCAN .... pg 244, 19 Sept 1849, list of sales

    woman Nancy, Mary & child George to James H. BROWNING; boy Henry to E.G. DUNCAN

Frederick DUNCAN .... pg 250, 18, 19 Sept 1849, list of sale

    Sandy, Robert to James H. BROWNING; Thornton to B.H. DUNCAN; Alsie, Juliet to James M. DUNCAN; Maria & child, Kitty to Benjamin H. DUNCAN; James, Felicia & child to William DORSEY; Harriet & child to William H. BROWNING

Henry JONES .... pg 252, 2 Sept 1840, will

    all negroes (except those left to my sons) to wife Millie JONES; Nelson, Sandy, Mary & her child Maria to son Henry G. JONES; Benjamin, Stephen, Caroline & her 2 children Henry & a younger child unnamed to son Moses R. JONES; after death of wife her negroes to be divided among daughters Lucinda ACKINS, Sarah ANDERSON, Elizabeth Ann PIERCE, & Tabitha GLASCOCK

Moses JEFFRIES .... pg 260, 24 July 1838, will

> boy Howard to son Daniel JEFFRIES after death or marriage of his mother Molly JEFFRIES; girl Elvira to daughter Lucy JEFFRIES after death or marriage of her mother Molly JEFFRIES

Henry JONES .... pg 267, 13 Sept 1852, inv & appr

> Edmund age 65, Alfred 39, George 26, Daniel 50, Rhody 55, Betsy 55, Olfilia & her 2 children, Juliana 17, Eveline 23, Rose 17, Rebecca 15, Margaret 14, Hamilton 12
>
> Nelson 35, Sandy 24, Mary 31 & child, Maria 13, Melissa 11, Malinda 9, Charlotte 6, Dallas 5 to Henry G. JONES; Stephen 27, Caroline 33, Henry 14, Addison 13 Bradford 11, Emily 9 to Moses R. JONES

Theoderick HUFF .... pg 271, 21 Feb 1852, inv & appr

> girl Maria

Silas FRISTOE .... pg 273, 6 Oct 1852, sale of negroes

> girl age 9 to Thomas GOLDING; girl age 7 to William H. MILLER

John PEYTON .... pg 283, 20 May 1852, will

> woman Frances to son Howard PEYTON in trust for daughter Lucy HUFFMAN; man Addison to son Howard PEYTON in trust for daughter Elizabeth PEYTON

John PEYTON .... pg 285, 18 Nov 1852, inv & appr

> man Addison, woman Frances

Elizabeth I. LANE .... pg 291, 27 Dec 1852, div of slaves

> ...interest in said slaves except Bob, Jack, Sawney, Nancy, Ella, Daniel, Sally, Lavinia & divide them upon death of Elizabeth I. LANE among... John G. LANE in his own right & as trustee of Martha F. SCOTT with husband John F. SCOTT, Mary Ellen LANE,

Julie JETT wife of James JETT, M. Elvira KELLY wife of Monroe KELLY, & Eliza L. SLAUGHTER wife of Montgomery SLAUGHTER .... pg 294, 1 Jan 1853

...except Jack, Sawney, Bob, Nancy & her children, Ella, Daniel, Sally & her child Lavinia to John G. LANE in his own right & as trustee of Martha F. SCOTT

Enoch age 28, Edward 26, Woodson 24, Charles Robert 22, Marshall 30, Madison, Sam 25, Manuel 18, Christopher 17, Austin 16, Bunson 14, Howard 10, Margaret 18, Amelia 16, Anarka 18, Harriet 14, Alcinda 12, Mary 8, Betsy 10, Adaline 23 & her children Dick 4, Henry 2, & Jefferson infant, Charlotte 40 & her children Fanny 4, Davy 2, & Martha infant, Caroline 52 & child Douglas 7, Catherine 20 & her children William 2 & Ann ½ year, old Sam, old Judy

Lot 1: Enoch, Charlotte & children Fanny, Davy, Martha, Manuel; Lot 2: Edward, Amelia, Christopher, Mary; Lot 3: Woodson, Catherine, William, Anna, Betsy, Caroline, Douglas; Lot 4: Charles Robert, Adaline, Dick, Henry, Jefferson, Harriet, Madison; Lot 5: Marshall, Margaret, Austin, Howard; Lot 6: Jim, Anarka, Bunson, Alcinda

Lot 1 to Montgomery SLAUGHTER; Lot 2 to James JETT; Lot 3 to Mary Ellen LANE; Lot 4 to Monroe KELLY; Lot 5 to John G. LANE trustee of Fanny SCOTT; Lot 6 to John G. LANE in his own right; old Sam to John G. LANE; old Judy, Madison to Monroe KELLY

Elijah AMISS .... pg 309, 29 Dec 1852, list of sales

man Randall to Richard COOPER; man Armistead to Benjamin D. SEAVELL; old woman Daphney to John M. SEAVELL; boy Nelson to Richard COOPER; Susan & child to James A. MENEFEE

James M. OBANNON.. pg 318, 14 Jan 1853, will

negroes to be equally divided between wife & children; wife's allotment to be divided among children at her death

Moses JEFFRIES ....pg 326, 10 Feb 1853, inv & appr

Marcus, Armistead, Duff, Noah, Milly, Hannah, Fanny

Samuel HARRIS .... pg 343, 5 May 1853, inv & appr

    Conrad age 27

Philip THORNTON .... pg 362, 18 May 1853, inv & appr

    37 negroes

John HOLLAND .... pg 363, 2 Oct 1849, will

    _alace, Amanda to daughter Louisa HOLLAND; Moses, Betty to daughter Lucy F. HOLLAND

Frances BURGESS .... pg 369, 20 Nov 1851, acct of sales

    child Phoebe, girl Charlotte to E.B. JACOBS; Mary & child, Jemima, Alex & child, Eliza to Thomas HUNT; boy Bob, girl Caroline to A.S. GRIGSBY; Edmund to Robert DEATHERAGE; Lucy, Sally's child, Malinda's child to C. BURGESS; boys Arthur, Middleton, girl Ellen to William H. JACOBS

Lewis JENKINS .... pg 373, 8 Sept 1853, inv & appr

    man Ben

John BROYLE .... pg 373, 6 Aug 1845, inv & appr

    girl

John M. OBANNON .... pg 376, 16 Feb 1853, inv & appr

    Richard, Milly, Hiram, John, Charles, Silvy, Maria, Billy, Martha, Lucy, Eliza, Sawny, Hamilton, Jack, Nimrod, Adolphus, Dolly, James

James HITT .... pg 380, 12 Oct 1853, will

    slaves not to be sold; boy Charles to daughter Jane, wife of William EMBREY; 5 slaves to be hired out during the life of wife Melinda

John I. BROWNING .... pg 384, 12 Dec 1853, will

    girl Helen to daughter Jane CAMPBELL wife of Walker CAMPBELL

Turner BARBEE ....pg 390, 17 Jan 1854, agreement

    slaves to be divided between Robert M. BARBEE, Henry C. BARBEE, Beal A. BARBEE, Mary J. PAGE, & Martha A. HAND

Turner BARBEE .... pg 391, 28 Apr 1834, trust deed

    Benjamin age 70, Caty 70, David 50, Agnes 50, Emanuel 22, Amanda 23, Eastham 14, Ann 12, Reuben 9, Joseph 21

    Lot 1: Emanuel, Benjamin to Robert M. BARBEE; Lot 2: Amanda to Mrs. Mary J. PAGE; Lot 3: Eastham, Joseph to Mrs. Martha A. HAND; Lot 4: Ann, David to Henry C. BARBEE; Lot 5: Reuben, Agnes, Caty to Beal A. BARBEE

Turner SETTLE .... pg 393, 26 Oct 1853, inv & appr

    man Taliafero

James HITT .... pg 395, 13 Mar 1854, appr of slaves

    Squire, Milton, Marshall, Sandy

John I. BROWNING .... pg 395, 17 Jan 1854, inv & appr

    men Charles, Henry; girl Helen willed to Jane CAMPBELL

Hannah L. BROOKE .... pg 397, 27 Dec 1853, inv & appr

    negro hire (bonds)

Amanda B. AMISS .... pg 407, 27 Dec 1853, inv & appr

    Ginny, Emily, boys Henry, Manuel

John I. BROWNING .... pg 409, 19 Jan 1854, acct of sales

    man Charles to Richard H. BROWNING; man Henry to Fayette BROWNING

John BROYLES .... pg 414, 8 Aug 1845, list of sales

    girl to Mr. __ REID

Abner SIMS .... pg 417, 24 Feb 1854, will

    Sally, Henry, Burwell & others of her selection to Mildred SAUNDERS, slaves to be sold at her death

John W. POPHAM .... pg 418, 20 Apr 1854, will

    slaves to wife Elizabeth Ann POPHAM, slaves to be sold to children at her death

James M. WOODARD .... pg 419, 12 June 1854, inv & appr

    girl Mary

Betsey W. GIBSON .... pg 424, 17 July 1854, will

    Nelly, Cyrus to granddaughter Julian G. MYERS; Daniel to be sold

Reuben BROOKE .... pg 426, 17 Sept 1854, will

    man Joseph, girl Mary to wife

.... pg 426, 19 Sept 1854, codicil

    girl Sarah to daughter Julia; girl Bell to daughter Virginia

Richard CORLEY .... pg 427, 28 Sept 1854, will

    slaves are not to be sold; old women Polly & Jenny to choose masters and be free

James SLOANE .... pg 429, 13 Sept 1853, will

    man William, Judy & her infant child Daniel, boy Richard to Sarah C. SMITH daughter of Sophia SMITH; man French, woman Jerusha, girl Emily to Silas DANIEL son of Henry DANIEL; women Zilphey, Hannah, girl Mary, man Woodson to James H. BROWNING; woman Mourning to Amanda GRIMSLEY wife of Aldridge GRIMSLEY

Samuel HARRIS .... pg 430, 5 Jan 1854, inv & appr

man Coon

Samuel HARRIS .... pg 431, 13 Jan 1854, acct of sales

man to James W. BRAGG

Abner SIMMS .... pg 431, 29 Aug 1854, inv & appr

man Burwell, woman & child Matilda, girls Elizabeth, Sally, Catherine, boys Henry, Jim

Abner SIMMS .... pg 433, 31 Aug 1854, acct of sale

woman & child to Willis BROWNING; girl Sally to W.C. CHEEK; boy Jim to C.W. BROWNING; Elizabeth, Catharine, boy Henry to Mildred SAUNDERS

Moses JEFFRIES .... pg 438, 18 Dec 1844, div of slaves

boy Howard, man Duff to Daniel JEFFRIES; girl Elvira, boy Armistead to Lucy JEFFRIES; woman Hannah to George JEFFRIES; woman Milly to Joseph REID assignee of Harrison JEFFRIES; boy Noah to Jesse JEFFRIES; man Marcus, girl Frances to James HITT & his wife Nancy nee JEFFRIES; old woman to Daniel JEFFRIES & Miss Lucy JEFFRIES

James SLOANE .... pg 444, 19 Dec 1854, inv & appr

man William, Judy & son Daniel, boy Richard willed to S.C. SMITH; man French, woman Jerusha, girl Emily willed to Silas DANIEL; old woman Zilphey, girls Hannah, Mary, man Woodson willed to James H. BROWNING; old woman Mourning willed to Mrs. GRIMSLEY; John 10 months old

Reuben BROOKE ....pg 446, 30 Nov 1854, inv & appr

 man Joe, boy Jack, women Elisa, Mary, Sarah, girl Bell

Reuben BROOKE ....pg 448, 15 Dec 1854, acct of sale

 woman Eliza to Richard N. HERNDON; boy Jack to Gobden S. MELLON

Peyton ANDERSON ....pg 449, 20 Nov 1854, inv & appr

 man Henry, women Lizza, Mary, men Alfred, Frank, Willis, boys Peter, Lewis, George, man John, woman Ophilia, girl Isabella

Richard CORLEY .... pg 457, 30 Dec 1854, sale of slaves

 girl Mary Frances to James H. MEYERS; Caroline & child to J.L. RICE; boy Ashby to James H. DOWNING; boy Jack to D.H. BEGGARLY

William RIVERCOMB .... pg 459, 12 Dec 1854, inv & appr

 Amy age 23 & her 3 children Mary 3, Frank 2, & Jimmy 1

WILL BOOK D
1855-1865

Maria WILSON .... pg 1, 9 July 1855, inv & appr

men Szdno, Charles, Adolphus, Maria & 2 children Margaret & George, girl Hetty, boy Henry, Harriet & 2 children Mary & Peter, boys Fendelon, Dick, Billy, Louisa & 3 children __ne, Daniel, & Betty, woman Kezia

Richard CORLEY .... pg 5, 5 Dec 1855, inv & appr

Laura & child Andrew, boys Henderson, McDaniel, girl Ann, boy Lomax, girl Eveline, man Henry, boy Daniel, girls Mary, Hannah, Willey, Caroline & child, woman Mary Frances, boys Jack, Ashby, Eliza & child, boy Edward, girl Nancy, boy William, Sarah & child Mary Jane, boys Philip, Oswelo, girl Matilda, Harriet & child Polly, girl Mary, Louisa, Thomas, Lewis, Sophia & child Thornton, Catharine, Lewis Edward, Delila, Eliza, Rachel, Roxaline, Roberta

Richard CORLEY .... pg 7, 11 Dec 1854, div of slaves

...after first excluding the emancipated slaves, 1/3 of the slaves of the said testator for the use & benefit of the testator's widow & then divide the residue thereof except such as may be sold...

Laura & child Andrew, Henderson, McDaniel, Ann, Lomax, Eveline, Henry, Daniel, Mary, Hannah, Willey to widow; Caroline & child, Mary Frances, Jack, Ashby to be sold; Eliza & child, Edward, Nancy, William to Charlotte MORRISON wife of John A. MORRISON; Sarah & child Mary Jane, Philip, Oswelo, Matilda to John Thomas CORLEY, Mary Catharine CORLEY, & Charlotte Sophrine CORLEY, children of John CORLEY dec'd; Harriet & child Polly, Mary, Louisa, Thomas, Lewis to James Richard HEATON & Martha Ann HEATON children of Betsy Ann HEATON daughter of testator; Sophia & child Thornton, Catherine, Delila, Lewis, Edward, Eliza to Mary F. MORRISON wife of Russel MORRISON; Rachel, Roxaline, Roberta to Jane MURPHY wife of Elias MURPHY

James M. OBANNON .... pg 16, 31 Oct 1855, div of slaves

>1/3 allotted to Lucy M. SMITH nee OBANNON wife of Cornelius SMITH

John COWGILL .... pg 17, 11 Aug 1855, will

>slaves to be sold

Frances WHITESCARVER .... pg 19, 16 Nov 1855, inv & appr

>Elias, Peter

Frances WHITESCARVER .... pg 20, 16 Nov 1855, acct of sales

>Elias to R.A. WHITESCARVER; Peter to L.C. WHITESCARVER

Alfred DEARING .... pg 22, 5 Feb 1856, will

>all my slaves except my advancements to my sons to wife Ann DEARING & at her death to be divided among 5 sons & grandson Alfred D. RHODES

George JETT .... pg 24, 29 Jan 1856, inv & appr

>Ben age 41, Sam 21, Shack 43, Peg 52, boy Frank

James M. WOODARD .... pg 26, 28 Apr 1854, list of sales

>girl to James JOHNSON

John AMISS .... pg 29, 16 Oct 1854, will

>Horace, Reuben, Oscar, Caesaran, Sarah Ann to wife Lavinia AMISS; woman Malinda to daughter Polly SCOTT

George JETT .... pg 31, 29 Jan 1856, list of sales

>Mishack hired to John L. RICE; Peggy hired to Samuel DOWDEN

Berryman HUGHES..............................pg 36, 6 Aug 1856, will

woman Cinderella to Thomas HUGHES Jr. in trust for niece Henrietta MOORE; girl Delia to Thomas HUGHES Jr. in trust for niece Lucy CURTIS; woman Nelly to Thomas HUGHES Jr. in trust for niece Mary CALVERT; girl Eliza to niece Rachel HUGHES; old negroes to nephew Thomas HUGHES

William CORBIN..............................pg 37, 28 Aug 1856, inv & appr

boy Thornton, woman Dinah

John AMISS..............................pg 42, 8 Aug 1856, inv & appr

men Jim, George, Horace, women Maria, Agnes, Kesiah & child, boys Moses, Ben, Aaron, Oscar, Reuben, Charles, Bob, Thomas, Jackson, Emanuel, Harriet & child Fanny, Esther & child Margaret, woman Cesar Ann, men Nat, John Henry, girl Sarah Ann, boy Gabriel

John N. POPHAM.............................. pg 48, 6 Jan 1855, inv & appr

boys Henry, Bill, Lewis, Primus, woman Vina, girl July, boys George, Samuel

William JONES..............................pg 49, 14 Oct 1856, inv & appr

George age 22

William CORBIN.............................. pg 60, 29 Aug 1856, list of sales

man Thornton to John SCOTT; woman Dina to Mrs. N. CORBIN

Armistead CORBIN..............................pg 62, 20 Oct 1856, inv & appr

men John Gordon, John Wilson, George Gordon, George Shelton, Seth, Lucy & 2 children, Maria & child, women Sally, Harriet, girls Jane, Celia, Susan, Eliza, Aggy, Louisa, Mildred, Judy, boys Albert, Dick, Moses, Aaron old women Sooky, Grace

Robert JONES ....pg 64, 14 Oct 1856, inv & appr

>men Carter, Jared, Jack, boy Lewis, Mary & child

Mrs. Lavina AMISS .... pg 70, 2 Sept 1856, property kept

>Horace, boys Oscar, Reuben, woman Caesaran, girl Sarah Ann

Susan PRIEST ....pg 71, 24 Oct 1856, inv & appr

>boy Humphrey, woman Mariah

John COWGILL ....pg 73, 25 Feb 1856, inv & appr

>William, George, Moses, Thornton, Henry, Strother, Ginny, Adaline, boy Jack

John COWGILL .... pg 76, 6 & 7 Mar 1856, list of sales

>man William to Alfred COWGILL; man George to Mary SEDWICK; man Moses to Richard L. RUDASILLA; man Thornton to Butler CORDER; man Henry to Eastham JORDAN; man Strother to Elias CORDER; girl Adaline to James B. SEDWICK; boy Jack to Nathan CORDER; woman Jane to Mary SEDWICK

Robert JONES .... pg 82, 3 Nov 1856, list of sales

>man Jared to Charles SMITH; Mary & child to Mrs. L.A. BARNES; boy Lewis to Richard N. BURKE; man Jack to Charles BROWN

Washington A. MARLOW .... pg 89, 8 Dec 1856, inv & appr

>Lewis age 28, Gilbert 26, Fielding 50, Elijah 55, Arch 80, Reuben 12, Lucy & 2 children Roy 8 & Jake 5, Eliza 40, Elias 45, Winney 90

James D. BROWNING .... pg 97, Aug 1856, list of sales

>girl Mary Eliza, man Strother to G.E. BROWNING; girl Isabella to B.F. EASTHAM; girl Lucy to B.F. MILLER; boy French to William J. SILLARD; man Lewis to A.H. BROWNING; man Darmet to B.F.

EASTHAM; Ellen & child to James COWGILL; woman Aga to Alfred COWGILL; man Strother to G.J. BROWNING

James SLOANE .... pg 101, 21 Dec 1854, list of sales

child John to Mrs. Sarah C. SMITH

William FLETCHER .... pg 103, 26 Mar 1856, will

little Jack, Sarah, Adaline, John Glen, Burkett, Malinda, Sarah Catharine & Sarah sucking child, Jerry, little Sally & little Sally sucking child Sophia, Till, big Sally, Bertha, Judy, Umphry, Burrella, Alfred to wife Elizabeth FLETCHER; 11 negroes to son James W. FLETCHER; negroes to son John T. FLETCHER & son Hamilton S. FLETCHER (10) to equal James W. FLETCHER's negroes

Maria WILSON ....pg 105, 22 Nov 1855, acct of sales

old woman Molly to Richard THORNHILL; Sidney to B.F. ROWLES; Charles to W.C. CHEEK; Adolphus to Charles YATES; Maria & 2 children, Henry to Richard THORNHILL; Hetty, Harriet & 2 children, Billy, Dick to Eveline WILSON; Fendelon to Henry SPARKS; Matilda to Washington WILSON; Louisa & 4 children to Thomas DEATHERAGE

Susannah GRIGSBY ....pg 113, 15 Sept 1847, will

woman Rose to Bazil GRIGSBY & Jane MILLER nee Jane GRIGSBY

Joseph AMISS .... pg 123, 17 Mar 1857, will

Wheden, Alsey, Sarah Ann & her children to wife Miriam AMISS; Jane & her 2 children, Seth to executor John F. AMISS in trust for daughter Mary Ann wife of George MOORE; Mariah & her 2 children, Andrew to executor John F. AMISS in trust for daughter Adeline C. HUME wife of Benjamin L. HUME; Julia to executor John F. AMISS in trust for daughter Arbelia RHODES wife of Edward RHODES; Arthur sold by Edward RHODES

.... pg 125, 17 Mar 1857, codicil

...Bob has died & supply his place with another slave; Bill a child of Sarah Ann to son John T. AMISS in trust for daughter Harriet G. WALTER; said boy Bill be taken from the slaves given to wife Mariam AMISS

James BASLY .... pg 126, 25 May 1858, inv & appr

Shadrach age 34, Moses 70, Sarah 79, Emily 38, Henry 12, John 10, Frank 3

John GRIGSBY .... pg 127, 19 May 1858, inv & appr

Charles age 37, Francis 31 & child 1 year old, Amanda 12, Martha 10, Bengalina 8

W.A. MARLOW .... pg 131, 7 Jan 1857, list of sales

Gilbert to Samuel GIBBONS; Lewis to Levi MARLOW; Eliza to Thomas N. ASHBY; Fielding, Roy, Jake to Mrs. MARLOW; Elijah to J. JETT; Elias to J.H. DOWNING; Reuben to W. _ILLARD; Arch to William ROBERSON; Lucy & 2 children to W.H. HICKERSON; Winney to T.W. ASHBY

Susannah GRIGSBY .... pg 134, 9 Nov 1858, inv & appr

old woman Rose

Joseph CORBIN .... pg 140, 22 Jan 1855, will

negroes to wife Hannah CORBIN to be sold at her death

Joseph CORBIN .... pg 142, 26 Feb 1859, inv & appr

woman Eliza, girl Molly

Robert HUDSON .... pg 152, 4 July 1859, inv & appr

Winney & child, girls Alice, Maria, Melinda, Ellen & child, men Henry, Gilbert

William TANNEHILL ....pg 165, 7 Nov 1859, inv & appr

 Delice & child, boy Jack

John BRADY .... pg 184, 5 Apr 1855, will

 slaves to wife Ann N. BRADY, at her death slaves to be divided among children

Joseph CORBIN ....pg 186, 28 Feb 1859, List of sales

 woman Eliza to A.C. SURNDLIN; girl Molly to J.B. GORE

Catharine BURGESS ....pg 192, 7 Nov 1859, inv & appr

 men Henry, Elias, Icy & 2 children, Sally & child, girl Priscilla, boys Andrew, Robert

Catherine BURGESS .... pg 194, 8 Nov 1859, list of sales

 man Henry to Mrs. Ann CAMP; man Elias to Garner C. BURGESS; Sally & child to W.W. DEATHERAGE; Icy & 2 children to John RAWLES; girl Priscilla to GADDING; boy Andrew to BRAWNER; boy Bob to William DEARING

John MILLER .... pg 200, 27 Dec 1859, div of slaves

 old John & wife, old Isaac, old Mary to Mrs. J.B. JONES; old George to B.T. MILLER; old Thom to John MILLER; old Anthony to Mrs. WOOD; Sanford to B.F. MILLER

 Alpheus age 35, Galrice 35, Robert 30, Arthur 24, Brooks 23, Lewis 22, Jemagea 15, Jones 15, Daniel 12, Eliza 32 & child Jim 1 year, Mallery 8, Harriet 30 & child George 4, Ellen 25 & child George 3, Bunel 5, Bette 22 & child Turner 2, Caroline 16, Emily 22 & child 8 months old

 Alpheus, Eliza & child Jim to Mrs. Sarah WHEATLEY; Robert, Emily & child to Mrs. Lucy WOOD; Galrice, Betty, Turner to Henry MILLER; Arthur, Lewis to Jesse MILLER; Brooks, Mallery, Bunel to John MILLER: Jim, Ellen & child George to J.B. JONES; Jones, Harriet & child George to B.F. MILLER; Daniel, Caroline to John J. SETTLE & Mrs. Elizabeth SETTLE

Hezekiah RICKETT .... pg 209, 21 Oct 1859, inv & appr

>man Jess, woman Mary

Hezekiah RICKETT .... pg 211, 11 June 1860, list of sales

>man Jess, girl Mary to John C. RICKETT

John BRADY .... pg 214, 11 June 1860, inv & appr

>boy Peter, Fannie & child Dallas, girl Lutisa, boys Dick, John, Ann & child Henry

Catherine DEATHERAGE .... pg 218, _ Aug 1856, will

>girls Polly & Rebecca to be divided among sons William W., John Landy, George, & Robert DEATHERAGE & granddaughter Mary Catharine SEARS

Elizabeth KEMPER .... pg 220, 1 Dec 1855, will

>boy Arthur to be sold & to select his master

Jesse PULLEN .... pg 222, 2 Nov 1860, will

>Kesiah to be free after death of wife Nancy PULLEN

Ann L. CAMP .... pg 224, 21 Dec 1860, inv & appr

>Bartlett age 50, Esther 18, Ann 14

Thomas BALL .... pg 227, 20 Oct 1860, will

>Amanda and her children except her third child Alice to daughter Sarah Ellen BALL; Alice, girl Sally, Winney & her children, woman Fanny to daughter Martha A. FISHER; Adelaide & her children to daughter Mary A. BROWN; Julia & her children, old Amy to daughter Margaret E. PAYNE; Emily & her children, man Marshall to son John Thomas BALL

.... pg 229, 3 Nov 1860, codicil

negro bequeathed to daughter Sarah Ellen BALL to live with her mother in trust for daughter Sarah Ellen BALL

James M. JONES................................ pg 230, 21 Dec 1860, div of slaves

Lot 1: Harriet & her 3 children Frank, Laura, & Hannah, Louisiana, Albert, Behsmitt to Lucy A.M. JONES; Lot 2: Margaret & her 3 children Mason, Alfred, & infant, Virginia, Gustavis, Catherine, old Charlotte, old Ruthy, old Violette to B.G. JONES; Lot 3: Emily & her child Erelina, Eliza & her child Fanny, Polk, Aldridge, Ann, George to T.A. JONES

Jesse PULLEN ....pg 231, 7 Feb 1861, inv & appr

girl Margaret

Jesse PULLEN ....pg 234, 8 Feb 1861, list of sales

girl Margaret to John S. BUCKNER

Winston P. WHITESCARVER...............pg 235, 22 Feb 1861, inv & appr

boy Thornton, girl Ann, boys Frank, Thomas, Millie & child Silar

Elias CORKSEY .... pg 238, 21 Mar 1861, div of slaves

Celia age 53, Jerry 29, Bob 28, Ann 6, Arthur 5 to the widow's dower; Lot 1: Ben 24, Elzy 3 to John M. CORKSEY; Lot 2: Lewis 20 to Philip F. CORKSEY ; Lot 3: Charlotte 31, Henry 14 to James W. CORKSEY; Lot 4: Jane 32 & child, George 24 to Phebe A. CORKSEY; Lot 5: Betty 20 & child to Caroline B__LING & her trustee P. F. CORKSEY

Charles TURLEY .... pg 243, 27 Dec 1859, inv & appr

Moses age 62, Alfred 57, Jacob 41, Oscar 3_, Alfred Jr. 31, Cerner 23, Eli 21, Moses Jr. 19, Nea 17, Daniel 15, Dallas 13, John 9, David 6, Pendelton 5, Bentin 4, Frank 3, Mary 52, Harriet 26 & child, Mary Jane 17, Almarisa 3, Catherine 10, Maria 10, Luscin 8 (Lucien?),

Alcinda 26, Betty 12; to Nancy TURLEY widow: Nea 17, David 6, Eli 21, Jacob 41, Frank 3, Luscin8, Alcinda 26, Catharine 10

Thomas BALL.. pg 249, 1 Apr 1861, inv & appr

Amy age 65, Fanny 49, Marshall 37, Wallace 33, George 30, Amanda 28 & child, Betty 25 & child, Clara 20, Bob 16, Lavinia 10, Alice 8, Fanny 6, Patsy 3, Alexander 3, Ben 3

Reuben SLAUGHTER.......................... pg 250, 10 June 1861, inv & appr

Harry age 60, Dangerfield 50, John 28, Scott 23, Douglas 17, Lewis 28, Winney 52, Margaret 30 & 2 children Ben 2 & infant child, Rachel 15, Amy 11, Fanny 11

James P. DEAL ....pg 256, 8 July 1862, inv & appr

boy, woman & her __ children

Silas DEAVERS.. pg 258, 20 Mar 1862, will

Jevisha, Emily & her children to wife Mary Ann DEAVERS

Robert EASTHAM... pg 259, 15 Dec 1852, will

negroes at W.W. DEATHERAGE to be account of worth for wife Frances Catherine & daughter Virginia EASTHAM, Virginia to have choice of 1 negro; daughter Mary Mrs. GARDNER to share in estate

James HINSEN .... pg 263, 21 Jan 1863, will

boy in possession of Jane SINGLETON

George H. BAKER...................................pg 262, 17 Feb 1863, inv & appr

boy Robert, Charlotte & child William

Madison C. KLEIN .... pg 275, 5 Jan 1861, will

girl Annetta to be sold & to select her master/mistress; girl Mary, purchased by me 16 July 1856 of James GRAHAM, to John M. MILLER in trust for sister Catharine

Benjamin STRINGFELLOW .... pg 295, 31 Dec 1861, will

> boy Dennis, girl Alcinda to wife Susannah STRINGFELLOW; residue of slaves to be sold; boy Dennis, girl Alcinda to be sold at the death of my wife

Paul GATES .... pg 297, 10 Jan 1869, will

> boy William to daughter Mary G. BOWIN; woman Tabitha & her child Harriet to daughter Elizabeth M. HARRIS; man Daniel to son Paul W. GATES; girl Lavinia, man Bennett, woman Kisiah to son William T. GATES

William I. MENEFEE .... pg 298, 8 Mar 1862, will

> man Davy to nephew Gidean H. BROWN; Thom to brother Alexander T. MENEFEE

Dr. Mark REID .... pg 299, 25 Feb 1860, will

> Maria, Selas to daughter Sarah Jean CALANCH

Paul GATES .... pg 304, 19 Nov 1863, inv & appr

> Caleb age 22, Daniel 26, William 10, La_nia 8, Tabitha 31 & child 3, Kesiah 63, Bennette 38

George B. HISLE .... pg 311, 18 Jan 1864, inv & appr

> Connor George, Peter, Tuck, Frank, Lewis, Betty, Milly & girl

John ROMINE .... pg 327, 12 Aug 1864, inv & appr

> Ellen, Margaret, Martha, French, Fanny, Aaron, Turner, Mary, Mildred

Landon SILMAN ....pg 329, July 1851, will

>boy George to be free after death of Elizabeth SETTLE daughter of Francis SETTLE

Benjamin STRINGFELLOW .... pg 331, 3 Dec 1863, inv & appr

>Margaret age 25, Dennis 15, Mar 13, Alcinda 11, Laura 9, Jane 7, Amanda 5; hire of girl Alcinda to F._. MOORE

James HINSEN .... pg 338, 23 Mar 1863, inv & appr

>man Lewis, girls Martha, Ann, old woman Ginnie

John HINSEN... pg 340, 24 Mar 1863, list of sales

>man Lewis, woman Ann to A.J. SINGLETON; woman Martha to A. COWANS; woman Ginnie to William BUTLER

Lucinda RAWLINGS..............................pg 350, 12 Feb 1865, inv & appr

>man Frank hired

Henrietta S. BROWNING....................... pg 357, 20 Jan 1865, inv & appr

>woman Martha, Belle age 5, Jim 3, infant 7 months

Henrietta S. BROWNING...................... pg 357, 21 Mar 1865, acct of sale

>Martha & 3 children to B.F. MILLER

Francis MILLAN... pg 359, 13 May 1856, will

>girl Lucinda to Sabina MILLAN wife of Henry F. MILLAN & her children which I bought from H.F. MILLAN in 1855

Peggy FLETCHER.. pg 384, 9 June 1859, will

>girl Emald to niece Marie L. BROWNING; girl Mary Eliza to niece Sally N. BYWATER; women Adaline, Agnes to niece Martha A. SIMS; woman Jane to Sarah E. NELSON; man Charles, Sally, Francis & her child to nephew John T. FLETCHER

Mary A. MOORE............................... pg 408, 6 Jan 1866, inv & appr
   girl hired

James R. NELSON...........................pg 418, 24 Sept 1861, inv & appr
   man Dick age 52, woman 49, Albert 16, John 8, Esther 5 ½, Hannah 55

Peggy FLETCHER................. pg 450, 15 Dec 1865, list of notes or bonds
   servants hired

Mary A. WOOD.. pg 454, 22 Jan 1858, will
   man Lewis purchased by me of my son-in-law William MITCHELL late of Missouri to granddaughter Mary A. MORRISON

Jesse VANHORN.. pg 469, 16 Apr 1858, will
   servants Henry, Adam to 5 daughters: Martha A., Henrietta A., Mildred M., Maria L., Frances D.

Ludwell HITT ....pg 478, 31 Aug 1863, will
   slaves (if I have any) to be sold after death of wife Catherine HITT

OLD RAPPAHANNOCK COUNTY, VA
WILL BOOK 1
1665 - 1677

Look under Essex Co for Will Books of Old Rappahannack Co. Film # 7645969, digital # 1929899, items 3 & 4. Digital image 348 is the start of the index; digital image 353 is page 1.

Thomas Francis MORRISON .... pg 34, 15 June 1661, land grant

...for the transportation of 4 persons into this colony to William KILMAN (no indication if the 4 unnamed persons are indentured, slaves, or new colonists)

Richard LAWRENCE .... pg 67, 17 __ 1664

servant maid Rebs_a Sunderland to Michael HUGELL

Luke BILLINGTON .... pg 114, 13 Nov 1671, will

servants to wife Barbary BILLINGTON; man or woman servant to daughters Elizabeth, Jane, & Barbary on day of their marriage

Thomas WRIGHT .... pg 120, 28 May 1672, will

servants to wife Mary WRIGHT

William GODGKIN .... pg 134, 22 Mar 1671, will

servant John Boo__

Elizabeth BUTLER .... pg 136, 7 May 1673, will

boy to son Francis SLAUGHTER; man to be purchased for son H_anci_; woman to be purchased for brother BOOTH's children;...negroes...to be delivered to my children in kind...

Barbary BILLINGTON .... pg 164, 7 Aug 1674, will
   servants to daughter Barbary BILLINGTON

Richard LOES .... pg 174, 22 Apr 1675, will
   2 servants to son-in-law Jainel TACKETT; negroes, Indians, mullatoes to son-in-law Henry WILLIAMSON

Thomas COOPER .... pg 180, 29 July 1675, will
   servant Thomas

Robert PAYNE .... pg 187, 24 Mar 1671, will
   son John Robert's servants to be put on a plantation & managed for him

John PENN .... pg 206, 13 Jan 1676/7, will
   Mary Peyton to be free on my decease; servants to friend Thomas HANSAN

WILL BOOK 2
1677 – 1682

Henry BERRY .... pg 21, 30 Mar 167_, will

    Jane Stowe – unsure if servant or relative

Samuel SCOTT .... pg 49, 8 Sept 1677, will

    servant William Glew to Nicholas CONSTABLE for remainder of his serving time

Thomas HAWKINS .... pg 55, 8 Feb 1675, will

    one girl & one English servant to wife Francis HAWKINS

Rice JONES .... pg 70, 20 Nov 1676, will

    servants John Powell, Thomas Diett, 3 negroes Archery, Moses, Seniora to son John JONES; servants Robert Blackley, Zachariah Muller, Elizabeth Holland, 2 negroes James, Dido to son Rice JONES; lads Peter, Tom to daughter Anne JONES; child Kate to grandchild Margaret BROCHE daughter of John & Mary BROCHE to be nursed by her mother Dido until she be 3 years old then delivered to said grandchild

Richard BARBER .... pg 79, 4 May 1676, will

    boy to son Richard

Henry CLARK .... pg 108, 18 Apr 1678, will

    man servant, to be bought by executrix, to son-in-law Francis GORE

Thomas GOODRICH .... pg 116, 15 Mar 1678/9, Deed of Feoffment

    all the negroes, slaves, men & women…to Benjamin GOODRICH & Alice his wife (or maybe visa versa)

Thomas GOODRICH .... pg 118, 15 Mar 1678/9, will

> Will, Jermine, Nan & her daughter Mall & her son Ben, boy Will Brandy to son Benjamin; Saw, woman Cuthenah & her sucking child to son Joseph; Mary & her son George, boy Mannall to son Charles; Betty Watts, Thomas Evans, Fuller & her now sucking child to daughter Anne upon her marriage day or age 21; boys Isaac, Toby to son Peter when he becomes 21 years; boys Kyete, James to daughter Katherine upon her marriage day or at age 21

Richard TAYLOR .... pg 131, 8 Mar 1678/9, will

> servant

Alexander NEWMAN .... pg 137, 2 July 1679, will

> servants to son John NEWMAN & Paule WOODBRIDGE his guardian

Sarah WALKER .... pg 142, 28 Jan 1668, will

> boy Richard to daughter Anne PAINE; boy Pete to daughter Francis WALKER; girl Deborah to Jane WALKER; girl Suzanna to daughter Elizabeth WALKER; girl Mareay (Mary?) to Sarah WALKER at my decease; boy Palmar to daughter Easter WALKER on her marriage

Richard JONES .... pg 153, 3 Mar 1674, will

> 2 maid servants to wife; child which is my servant Susana Barance

Thomas WHITLOCK .... pg 157, 20 July 1680, probate London Court

> (these documents are confusing, read carefully)
>
> ...John WHITLOCK & Johanna HARRIS wife of Henry HARRIS...oaths...Anthony WHITLOCK is only son & child living of John WHITLOCK...James WHITLOCK of Virginia...
>
> .... pg 159, 12 July 1680
>
> Anthony WHITLOCK of Lambath...nephew & heir of Thomas WHITLOCK...late of Rapphannock River Plantation...servants of

uncle Thomas WHITLOCK...now belong to me...
....pg 163
end of probate most likely written in Latin

INDEX

_alace, 43
_ILLARD: W., 54
_illis, 1
Aaron, 3, 4, 6, 21, 27, 36, 51, 59
Abby, 6
Abraham, 5, 12, 26
Abram, 6
Absalom, 1, 3
Aby, 4
Ackin, 59
ACKINS: Lucinda, 40
Adaline, 3, 7, 21, 42, 52, 53, 60
Adam, 1, 6, 18, 61
ADAMS: Easter Verlinda, 11; John, 7
Addison, 9, 11, 23, 41
Adelaide, 33, 37, 56
Adolphus, 43, 49, 53
Aga, 53
Agga, 19, 38
Aggy, 15, 23, 28, 51
Agnes, 44, 51, 60
Albert, 2, 4, 16, 18, 20, 21, 31, 33, 51, 57, 61
Alcey, 39
Alcinda, 18, 21, 29, 30, 34, 35, 42, 58, 59, 60
ALCOCK: W.S., 39
Aldridge, 57
Alec, 12
Alecy, 2
Alex, 43
Alexander, 58
Alfred, 5, 8, 9, 16, 18, 19, 22, 25, 27, 41, 47, 53, 57
Alfred Jr., 57
Alice, 21, 36, 54, 56, 58
Allen, 8, 37
Almarisa, 57

ALMOND: Mann, 17; William K., 17
Alpheus, 55
Alsey, 53
Alsie, 40
Amanda, 1, 16, 19, 21, 25, 30, 35, 36, 37, 38, 43, 44, 54, 56, 58, 60
Amelia, 2, 42
AMISS: Amanda B., 44; Ann E., 39; Elijah, 24, 39, 42; H.W., 39; John, 50, 51; John F., 53; John T., 54; Joseph, 53; Lavina, 50, 52; Miriam, 30, 53, 54; Philip N., 10, 13, 20
Amy, 2, 6, 17, 18, 47, 56, 58
Anaky, 21
Anarka, 42
Anderson, 8
ANDERSON: Peyton, 47; Sarah, 40
Andreas, 29
Andrew, 3, 49, 53, 55
Angelina, 23, 38
Ann, 1, 3, 4, 6, 14, 18, 21, 25, 27, 29, 31, 33, 36, 37, 38, 39, 42, 44, 49, 51, 56, 57, 60
Ann Maria, 21
Anna, 42
Annaca, 13
Annake, 12
Anne, 6
Annetta, 58
Anthony, 1, 15, 16, 23, 24, 29, 55
Arch, 6, 9, 21, 52, 54
Archery, 65
Armistead, 2, 4, 6, 19, 20, 21, 39, 40, 42, 46

Arthur, 16, 38, 39, 43, 53, 55, 56, 57
Ashby, 47, 49
ASHBY: T.W., 54; Thomas N., 54
Austin, 2, 3, 21, 42
Aylett, 3, 12
B__LING: Caroline, 57
B_AGE: Joseph, 39
B_mkin: Gardner, 3
Bailer, 4, 26
Bailey, 22
BAINES: Elijah, 3
BAKER: George H., 58; J., 15
BALL: John T., 35; John Thomas, 56; Sarah Ellen, 56, 57; Thomas, 56, 58
BANNON: Hannah, 22
Barance: Susan, 66
Barbara, 25
BARBEE: Andrew R., 28; Beal A., 44; Henry C., 35, 44; Robert M., 44; Turner, 44
BARBER: Richard, 65
BARNES: Leonard, 6, 7; Mrs. L.A., 52
Bartlett, 39, 56
BARTON: J., 31
BASLY: James, 54
BASYE: Benjamin, 14, 19
BAURE: John, 9
Baylor, 2
Beck, 30
Becky, 37
Bedford, 14
BEGGARLY: D.H., 47
Behsmitt, 57
Belinda, 3
Bell, 45, 47
Belle, 39, 60
Ben, 6, 8, 21, 27, 31, 39, 43, 50, 51, 57, 58, 66
Bengalina, 54
Benjamin, 3, 26, 31, 36, 40, 44
Bennett, 17, 59

Bennette, 59
Bentin, 57
BERKLEY: Elizabeth, 25; Susan F., 25
BERRY: Henry, 65
Bertha, 53
Bet, 36
Bethana, 36, 37
Betsy, 3, 5, 16, 21, 25, 30, 38, 40, 41, 42
Betsy Ann, 17
Bette, 55
Betty, 1, 3, 7, 37, 43, 49, 55, 57, 58, 59, 66
Beverly, 14, 31
Bill, 13, 18, 20, 21, 22, 29, 51, 54
BILLINGTON: Barbary, 63, 64; Luke, 63
Billy, 8, 10, 27, 28, 33, 34, 39, 43, 49, 53
Bird, 1
Blackley: Robert, 65
BLACKWELL: Benjamin, 26; Winford, 14
Bob, 3, 5, 6, 18, 21, 27, 28, 38, 39, 41, 42, 43, 51, 54, 55, 57, 58
Boo__: John, 63
Books, 16
BOOTH, 63
BOWEN: Emily M.A., 11, 19; Gidean H., 27; Peter B., 15
BOWIN: Mary G., 59
BOWYER: George, 38
Bradford, 37, 41
BRADY: Ann N., 55; John, 25, 55, 56; Nancy, 25
BRAGG: James W., 46; Thomas, 5
BRANDOM: Ezekiel, 26, 27, 28
Brandy, 66; Will, 66
BRAWNER, 55
Brent: Lucy, 3

Broadus: Champ, 25
BROCHE: John, 65; Margaret, 65; Mary, 65
BROOKE: Hannah L., 44; Hannah S., 27; Reuben, 45, 47; William B., 24, 27
Brooks, 55
BROWN: Charles, 52; F.C. Newton, 33; Gidean H., 59; James M., 33; Mary A., 33, 56; Nicolas, 31; Thomas W., 33; William, 21, 25, 28; William P., 33, 35, 37; Willie E., 33
BROWNING: A.H., 52; C.W., 46; Cassandra, 22; E.S., 23; Fayette, 45; Frances L., 23; G.E., 52; G.J., 23, 53; Henrietta, 23; Henrietta S., 60; James A., 21; James D., 52; James H., 40, 46; John D., 22, 23, 30; John I., 44, 45; John R., 7; John S., 23; M__, 23; Margaret, 23; Marie L., 60; Mason, 18; Nicholas, 33; Richard H., 45; William H., 40; Willis, 21, 46
BROYLE: John, 43
BROYLES: John, 45
BUCKNER: John S., 18, 57
Bundy, 21
Bunel, 55
Bunson, 42
BURGESS: C., 43; Catharine, 55; Catherine, 38, 39, 55; Frances, 38, 39, 43; Garner C., 55
BURKE: Richard N., 52; W.H., 39
Burkett, 53
Burley, 26
Burnette, 6
Burrell, 23
Burrella, 53

Burwell, 45, 46
Butler, 5, 10
BUTLER: Ann, 15; Elizabeth, 12, 63; William, 60
BYWATER: Henry, 16; Robert H., 20, 28; Robert Henry, 23; Sally N., 60; Thomas R., 28; Thomas Richard, 20; William, 21
BYWATERS: Robert H., 34; Thomas, 34
Caesar, 39
Caesaran, 50, 52
CALANCH: Sarah Jean, 59
Caleb, 27, 59
Cally, 2
CALVERT: Mary, 51
CAMP: Ann, 39, 55; Ann L., 56
Campbell: Winney, 3
CAMPBELL: Jane, 44; Walker, 44
CARMEN: John W., 39
Caroline, 1, 4, 6, 8, 11, 16, 18, 20, 21, 23, 28, 33, 34, 39, 40, 41, 42, 43, 47, 49, 55
CARPENTER: Thomas, 21
Carson, 39
CARSON: Betty W., 20; Elizabeth A.E., 26; Elizabeth A.W., 25
Carter, 28, 52
CARTER: William W., 17
CARVER: B., 31
Cassa, 14
Cassey, 34
Cassy, 2, 4
Cate, 6
Catharine, 46, 49, 58
Catherine, 18, 21, 26, 33, 42, 46, 49, 57
Cato, 20
Caty, 5, 8, 10, 12, 16, 44
Celia, 3, 4, 5, 6, 7, 8, 23, 25, 29, 38, 51, 57
Cerner, 57

Cesar, 51
Cha_t_an, 14
Champ, 18, 25
Chancello, 40
Charity, 4, 6, 18, 21
Charity Ann, 14
Charles, 2, 3, 4, 5, 6, 7, 8, 14, 16, 17, 18, 19, 20, 21, 23, 25, 26, 27, 28, 34, 36, 37, 38, 43, 44, 45, 49, 51, 53, 54, 60
Charles Robert, 21, 42
Charlotte, 1, 2, 3, 4, 6, 7, 8, 21, 22, 23, 25, 27, 28, 29, 30, 39, 41, 42, 43, 57, 58
CHEEK: Dicy, 17; E., 18, 28; Elijah, 12, 17; George, 17, 18; Isabella, 17, 18; L., 18; Lawson, 17; Mary, 8; W.C., 46, 53
Chilton, 6
China, 34
Christopher, 21, 42
Cinderella, 51
Clara, 21, 27, 58
CLARK: Henry, 65
Clary, 1, 2, 4, 8, 19, 23, 36, 40
CLIZER: Martin, 33
Coleman, 2, 4, 7
Collin, 5, 8
Columbus, 11
COMWILL: Isham, 7
Connor George, 59
Conrad, 43
CONSTABLE: Nicholas, 65
Coon, 46
COONES: Robinson, 12
COOPER: Richard, 42; Thomas, 64
Cora, 29, 30, 36, 37
CORBIN: Armistead, 51; Hannah, 54; Joseph, 54, 55; Mrs. N., 51; Rebecca, 34, 38; Sarah, 34, 38; William, 51
CORDER: Bueler, 37; Butler, 52; Elias, 8, 37, 52; Elijah, 31; Elish, 31; Hannah, 30; Isham, 37; John, 30, 37; Martha, 31; Nathan, 31, 37, 52; Vincent, 30
CORDER Jr.: John, 31
CORKSEY: Elias, 57; James W., 57; John M., 57; Phebe A., 57; Philip F., 57
CORLEY: Charlotte Sophrine, 49; John, 49; John Thomas, 49; Mary Catharine, 49; Richard, 45, 47, 49
Cornelia, 21
COWANS: A., 60
COWGILL: Alfred, 38, 52, 53; Dolly, 35; Elizabeth, 30; James, 38, 53; John, 50, 52
COXE: Anne, 31
CROPP: Edwin A., 25; John, 17, 21
Cupid, 13
CUREE: John, 1
CURTIS: Lucy, 51
Cuthenah, 66
Cyrus, 45
Dallas, 36, 37, 41, 56, 57
Dangerfield, 58
Daniel, 1, 2, 4, 6, 8, 10, 11, 13, 14, 19, 21, 23, 24, 25, 26, 27, 29, 30, 35, 36, 41, 42, 45, 46, 49, 55, 57, 59
DANIEL: Henry, 46; Molly, 9; Nancy, 9; Silas, 46
Daphney, 16, 39, 42
Darmet, 52
Davenport, 5, 8
David, 2, 3, 4, 30, 44, 57, 58
Davis: Aaron P., 3; Richard, 3
Davy, 19, 29, 30, 31, 42, 59
Dawson, 1
DEAL: Allen L., 36; James, 36; James P., 58; Margaret, 36; Margaret Ann, 36; Peter, 36, 37; Robert, 36

DEARING: Alfina, 27; Alfred, 50; Ann, 50; William, 55
DEATHERAGE: Catherine, 56; Elizabeth, 40; George, 4, 8, 40, 56; John, 40; John Landy, 56; Mary W., 40; Mrs. C., 14; Philip, 40; Robert, 40, 43, 56; Thomas, 53; W.W., 55, 58; William, 19; William A., 40; William W., 56
DEAVERS: Silas, 58
Deborah, 66
Deck, 9
Delia, 8, 37, 38, 51
Delice, 55
Delila, 1, 2, 4, 26, 49
Delsey, 23
Delsy, 23
Denise, 12
Dennis, 5, 25, 59, 60
Diana, 6
Dianna, 38
Dicey, 39
Dick, 36, 38, 42, 49, 51, 53, 56, 61
Dicy, 17, 31, 39
Dido, 65
Diett: Thomas, 65
Dina, 51
Dinah, 1, 6, 51
DODSON: Samuel, 7; William, 7, 8
DODY: David S., 2
Dolly, 3, 25, 43
DORSEY: Margaret, 26; William, 40
Douglas, 42, 58
DOWDEN: Samuel, 50
DOWNING: J.H., 54; James H., 47
Drusilla, 19
Duff, 42, 46
Dulceny, 34
DUNCAN: B.H., 40; Benjamin H., 40; E.G., 40; Edmond, 2;

Edward P., 6; Eldridge, 2; Eldridge G., 6; Frederick, 2, 6, 40; George, 8, 9; Harrison, 2, 6; James M., 2, 40; Margaret, 28; Mary Ann, 2, 6, 9; Randolph, 2, 6; Susan, 31, 40; Susannah, 2, 6
Early, 6
Eastham, 44
EASTHAM: B.F., 52, 53; Benjamin F., 4; Bird, 2, 4; Branton, 4; Frances Catherine, 58; George, 4; John, 4; Lawson, 4; Mary Ann, 7; Philip, 4, 7; Robert, 4, 30; Susan Ann, 7; Virginia, 58
Edith, 39
Edmond, 1, 4, 13, 36
Edmund, 2, 4, 5, 6, 7, 14, 20, 33, 39, 41, 43
Edward, 6, 16, 21, 29, 34, 37, 42, 49
Edwin, 15
Edy, 20
EGGBORN: George, 3
Eldridge, 1
Eleanor, 3
Eleck, 6
Elena, 3
Eli, 31, 57, 58
Elias, 4, 6, 39, 50, 52, 54, 55
Elijah, 4, 52, 54
Elisa, 18, 47
Eliz, 7
Eliza, 3, 10, 15, 16, 17, 20, 21, 22, 25, 30, 33, 37, 39, 43, 47, 49, 51, 52, 54, 55, 57
Elizabeth, 2, 3, 4, 5, 6, 16, 19, 29, 30, 46, 65
Ella, 41, 42
Ellen, 2, 3, 6, 8, 9, 10, 11, 14, 16, 18, 19, 23, 24, 25, 26, 27, 31, 35, 36, 37, 38, 39, 43, 53, 54, 55, 59

Ellick, 21
Elmira, 34
Eloisa, 16
Eloya, 17
Elvira, 16, 31, 36, 41, 46
Ely, 2
Elzina, 14
Elzy, 29, 57
Ema_e, 39
Emald, 60
Emancipated: Celia, 5; Elmira, 34; Frederick, 22; George, 33, 60; Harriet, 33; Henrietta, 33; Jenny, 45; Kesiah, 56; Maria, 33; Martha, 5; Mary Peyton, 64; Pender, 33; Polly, 45; Ruthy, 5; Stepney, 33; Tom, 33
Emanuel, 10, 17, 25, 44, 51
EMBREY: Jane, 43; William, 43
Emily, 3, 5, 6, 8, 15, 16, 18, 19, 20, 21, 26, 30, 35, 39, 41, 44, 46, 54, 55, 56, 57, 58
Enoch, 2, 4, 21, 42
Erelina, 57
Esther, 3, 26, 39, 51, 56, 61
Evans: Thomas, 66
Eve, 4, 6, 18, 39
Evelene, 2, 6
Evelina, 2, 6, 7, 11, 20, 31, 37, 39
Eveline, 11, 18, 25, 31, 39, 41, 49
Facey, 29, 30
Fannie, 56
Fanny, 3, 5, 6, 7, 15, 17, 18, 20, 21, 25, 26, 28, 42, 51, 56, 57, 58, 59
Fanny _0, 10
FANT: Elizabeth, 40
FARROW: French, 3; William, 2, 3
Felicia, 17, 25, 40
Felissa, 2

Fendelon, 49, 53
Festus, 14
FICKLIN: George, 39
Fielding, 4, 6, 52, 54
Fillis, 1
Filliss, 6
FISHER: Lucy, 30; Martha A., 56; Mary, 30; Thomas H., 27, 30
FLETCHER: Elizabeth, 53; Hamilton S., 53; James W., 53; John T., 53, 60; Peggy, 60, 61; William, 53
FLINN: Charles H., 29
FOGG: Elias, 14
FOLEY: Elizabeth, 11; James, 11; Thomas, 6, 11
Fran, 9
Frances, 2, 3, 11, 16, 30, 36, 37, 41, 46
Francis, 25, 54, 60
Frank, 3, 4, 5, 10, 16, 17, 18, 21, 24, 25, 30, 33, 37, 38, 47, 50, 54, 57, 58, 59, 60
Franklin, 6, 11
Frederick, 1, 8, 22, 26
French, 2, 3, 9, 21, 23, 29, 31, 33, 39, 45, 46, 52, 59; George, 4
FRISTOE: Joseph, 33; Silas, 31, 35, 41
Fuller, 66
Furlong, 33, 37
Gabriel, 3, 16, 51
GADDING, 55
GAINES: W.H., 39
Galrice, 55
GARDNER: Mary, 58
Garret, 17
GATES: Paul, 59; Paul W., 59; William T., 59
GAUNT: Alpheus, 34, 38; Andrew, 34, 38; Daniel, 34, 38; Isaiah, 34, 38; William, 34, 38

Gayden, 20
Gena, 9
George, 1, 3, 4, 6, 9, 10, 11, 13, 14, 15, 16, 18, 19, 20, 21, 24, 29, 31, 33, 34, 35, 36, 37, 38, 40, 41, 47, 49, 51, 52, 55, 57, 58, 60, 66
George Washington, 21
Georgianna, 34
Gerdan: Joseph, 3
Getty: Caroline, 20
Gevin: Bob, 3
GIBBONS: Samuel, 54
GIBSON: Betsy W., 45; Elizabeth W., 7; Mary, 13; Miner, 15; Moses, 7, 14, 15
Gilbert, 2, 4, 20, 21, 27, 52, 54
Ginnie, 60
Ginny, 44, 52
GIVENS: John, 31
GLASCOCK: Tabitha, 40
Glew: William, 65
GODGKIN: William, 63
Goldam: Negro trader, 35
GOLDING: Thomas, 37, 41
GOODRICH: Alice, 65; Benjamin, 65; Thomas, 65, 66
Gordan: John, 3
Gordon: George, 51; John, 51; John R., 3
GORE: Francis, 65; J.B., 21
GORE J.B., 55
Grace, 3, 51
GRAHAM: James, 59
Gray: Charles, 3
GRAY: Richard, 5
GREEN: A.F., 39; George James, 29; James, 22, 26; James George, 34; Moses, 28
GRIFFIN: Thomas, 4
GRIGSBY: A.S., 43; Bazil, 53; Henry, 8; Jane, 53; John, 54; Susannah, 53, 54

GRIMSLEY: Aldridge, 46; Amanda, 46; Mrs., 46
GROVES: Elizabeth, 34, 38
Gustavis, 57
Guy, 9
H_anci_, 63
Hagar, 15
Hamilton, 41, 43
Hammet, 36, 37
HAND: Martha A., 44; Thomas, 4
HANDSUCKER: Sarah, 30
Haney, 12, 18
Hannah, 1, 2, 3, 5, 6, 7, 9, 18, 20, 27, 36, 38, 42, 46, 49, 57, 61
Hanney, 22
HANSAN: Thomas, 64
Hansborough, 31
Hanson, 30
Harper, 21
Harriet, 2, 3, 5, 6, 7, 8, 9, 11, 16, 21, 23, 26, 28, 29, 30, 33, 34, 35, 36, 37, 40, 42, 49, 51, 53, 55, 57, 59
HARRINGTON: George W., 35; Peggy, 35; Susan E., 35
Harris, 9; Jack, 3
HARRIS: Elizabeth M., 59; Henry, 66; Johanna, 66; Samuel, 43, 46
Harrison, 8
Harry, 4, 6, 18, 19, 25, 28, 33, 58
HAWES: Aylett, 1, 3, 7; Walker, 2
HAWKINS: Frances, 65; Nancy, 10, 12; Thomas, 65
HAYNES: Rhoda, 15
HAYNIE: Anthony, 10, 17; George Anna, 17; Lucretia A., 17; Rhoda, 17; Richard A., 17; Sarah, 3; Sarah E., 17; Thadeus, 17

HEATON: Betsy Ann, 49; James Richard, 49; Martha Ann, 49
HEINSEY: Benjamin F., 31
Helen, 2, 44
Henderson, 37, 49
Hene, 29
Henny, 17, 18, 38
Henrietta, 3, 10, 16, 18, 25, 33, 35
Henry, 1, 2, 3, 4, 5, 6, 8, 9, 10, 11, 12, 15, 17, 18, 19, 20, 21, 26, 27, 29, 31, 33, 36, 37, 38, 39, 40, 41, 42, 44, 45, 46, 47, 49, 51, 52, 53, 54, 55, 56, 57, 61
HERNDON: Richard N., 47
HERRINGTON: Zadock, 35
Hester, 17, 27, 39
Hester Ann, 39
Hetty, 49, 53
HICKERSON: W.H., 54
HINSEN: James, 58, 60; John, 60
Hiram, 43
HISLE: Agnes, 25; Champ, 25; George, 25; George B., 59; Jesse, 25; John P., 25; Robert, 24, 25; Sam, 25; Samuel, 25; Thomas, 25
HITT: Catherine, 61; James, 43, 44, 46; Ludwell, 61; Nancy, 46
Holland: Elizabeth, 65
HOLLAND: John, 43; Louisa, 43; Lucy F., 43
HOPKINS: John, 5
HOPPER: John, 23, 30, 38; Joshua, 22, 29, 30
HOPPER Sr.: Joshua, 23
Horace, 6, 21, 39, 50, 51, 52
Howard, 5, 8, 25, 26, 33, 41, 42, 46
HUDSON: Alfred, 26; Armistead, 26; Elizabeth, 26, 27; John W., 26; Joshua, 26; Robert, 26, 27, 54; Susan, 26
HUFF: Cornelius, 29; Theoderick, 40, 41
HUFFMAN: Lucy, 41
HUGELL: Michael, 63
HUGHES: Berryman, 51; Boneman, 3; John S., 34; Rachel, 51; Thomas, 1, 3, 51
HUGHES Jr.: Thomas, 51
HUME: Adeline C., 53; Benjamin L., 53
Humphrey, 2, 4, 52
HUNT: Thomas, 43
Icy, 55
Isaac, 1, 2, 3, 6, 9, 16, 20, 22, 23, 34, 55, 66
Isabella, 5, 9, 13, 17, 21, 47, 52
Isham, 23
Ivy, 3
Jack, 1, 3, 4, 6, 8, 12, 14, 18, 19, 21, 24, 25, 29, 34, 36, 37, 40, 41, 42, 43, 47, 49, 52, 53, 55
Jackson, 12, 16, 28, 37, 51
JACKSON: Daniel, 37; Polly, 31
Jacly, 38
Jacob, 5, 8, 11, 13, 17, 20, 21, 57, 58
JACOBS: E.B., 43; William H., 43
Jake, 52, 54
Jam, 1
James, 2, 3, 6, 7, 12, 14, 20, 21, 23, 26, 27, 37, 39, 40, 43, 65, 66
Jamima, 39
Jane, 2, 3, 5, 9, 10, 12, 18, 21, 22, 25, 27, 28, 30, 31, 36, 39, 51, 52, 53, 57, 60, 65
Jane Stowe, 65
Jaqueline, 31
Jared, 2, 52
Jarred, 23

Jarrott, 22
Jaseh, 28
JASPER: Daniel, 8; Mary, 8; Mildred, 8; Robert, 8
Jefferson, 12, 42
Jeffrey, 3
JEFFRIES: Celia, 11; Daniel, 41, 46; F.M., 37; Frances M., 8; Francis M., 4; George, 46; Harrison, 46; Jane, 8; Jemima, 4, 5, 8; Jesse, 46; John, 4, 5, 8, 9; Louisa, 8; Louiza, 4; Louzia, 5; Lucy, 41, 46; Molly, 41; Moses, 41, 42, 46; Nancy, 11, 46; Reuben, 11
Jeffry, 29, 30
Jemagea, 55
Jemima, 19, 20, 26, 43
Jenetta, 25, 26
JENKINS: Lewis, 43
Jennette, 19
Jennifer, 30
Jenny, 3, 10, 11, 45
Jermine, 66
Jerrett, 13
Jerry, 2, 20, 53, 57
Jerusha, 45, 46
Jess, 2, 56
Jesse, 3, 6, 7, 8, 11, 29, 34
JETT: George, 50; J., 54; James, 42; Julie, 42; Susannah, 37
Jevisha, 58
Jim, 1, 3, 6, 14, 18, 21, 22, 24, 25, 27, 39, 42, 46, 51, 55, 60
Jimmy, 47
Jincess, 7, 8
Jinnie, 39
Jinny, 1, 13, 14, 16, 39
Joanna, 30
Joe, 1, 3, 6, 21, 35, 39, 47
Joe Lewis, 21
John, 3, 5, 9, 10, 13, 14, 16, 18, 22, 26, 27, 28, 31, 36, 37, 38, 43, 46, 47, 51, 53, 54, 55, 56, 57, 58, 61, 63, 65
John Glen, 53
John Henry, 51
Johnson: Benjamin, 3
JOHNSON: James, 50; Peter, 39
JOHNSON Jr.: William, 18
Jones, 21, 22, 25, 55; Lewis, 3; Rosanna, 3
JONES, 18; Anne, 65; B.G., 57; Charles E., 18, 24; Charles Eastham, 19; David L., 7; Eliza, 15; Elizabeth, 18, 19; et al, 19; George W., 18, 24; George William, 19; H.G., 39; Henry, 40, 41; Henry G., 40, 41; J.B., 55; James M., 57; John, 65; Lawson B., 18; Lawson Bird, 24; Lawson Byrd, 19; Lucy A.M., 57; Lucy M., 18; Lucy Margaret, 19, 24; Mary V., 18; Mary Virginia, 19; Millie, 40; Moses R., 40, 41; Mrs. J.B., 55; Rice, 65; Richard, 66; Robert, 28, 52; Rodham, 11; Sarah E., 18, 19; Sarah Elizabeth, 19; T.A., 57; Thomas, 10; William, 51; William E., 7, 18, 19; William R., 13
Jordan, 1
JORDAN: Absalom, 4; Eastham, 35, 52; Mary, 1; Sarah G., 1
Joseph, 3, 19, 44, 45
Joshua, 5, 24, 25
Juda, 4, 22, 27
Judah, 9
Jude, 2, 8, 18
Judson, 26
Judy, 3, 5, 10, 20, 21, 42, 45, 46, 51, 53
Julia, 33, 53, 56

Julia Ann, 2
Julian, 31
Juliana, 41
Julianna, 16
Juliet, 16, 27, 40
July, 51
Kate, 4, 36, 65
Katy, 5, 16
KEITH: America J., 13; Caroline M., 13; Eliza Ann, 13; Judith, 13; Louisa T., 13; Mary, 13; Peyton, 13
Keller, 3
Kelly, 7
KELLY: Elvira M., 42; Monroe, 42
KEMPER: Elizabeth, 56
KENDALL: Frances, 5; Melinda, 5
KENNARD: David, 16
Kesiah, 51, 56, 59
Kezia, 49
Keziah, 5
KILMAN: William, 63
KINNARD: Daniel, 16
Kisiah, 59
Kitty, 1, 3, 21, 40
Kizziah, 21
KLEIN: Madison C., 58
KNIGHT: L.H., 31, 35; S.H., 31
Kyete, 66
La_nia, 59
LALE: John, 9, 12
Landford, 20
LANE: Elizabeth I., 41; John G., 22, 41, 42; Mary Ellen, 41, 42; William A., 21
LATHAM: Mary C. AMISS, 20; R.C., 39
Laura, 49, 57, 60
Lavina, 3, 14
Lavinia, 21, 41, 42, 58, 59
LAWRENCE: Richard, 63
Leah, 21, 24, 27

LELLARD: Benjamin, 12
LETT: James, 31; John, 31
LETT Sr.: John, 31
Letty, 3, 11, 14, 21, 24
Levi, 14, 15, 16, 23, 28, 34
Levina, 11, 19
Lewis, 3, 5, 7, 12, 15, 16, 17, 18, 19, 20, 21, 22, 23, 24, 25, 28, 30, 33, 34, 36, 37, 38, 47, 49, 51, 52, 54, 55, 57, 58, 59, 60, 61
Lewis Edward, 49
Lib, 26
Lige, 6, 36
Lilly, 3
Littleton, 26
Lizza, 47
Lizzy, 20, 21
LOES: Richard, 64
Logan, 9
Lomax, 49
London, 9
Louis, 14
Louisa, 3, 9, 21, 24, 30, 38, 49, 51, 53
Louisiana, 57
Louiza, 5
Luce, 4
Lucien, 57
Lucinda, 3, 5, 9, 10, 15, 17, 20, 25, 38, 60
Lucretia, 25
Lucus, 14
Lucy, 1, 2, 3, 4, 5, 6, 8, 17, 21, 23, 25, 36, 37, 39, 43, 51, 52, 54
Lucy Ann, 3, 7, 16, 18, 22, 28, 34
Luscin, 57, 58
Lutisa, 56
Lydia, 1, 5, 21, 24, 25
MADDOX: James, 35
Madison, 5, 12, 16, 21, 37, 42; David, 3
Madlum, 31

Mahala, 6
Mahilah, 4
MAJORS: Sarah, 35
Malary, 3
Mald, 1
Malinda, 14, 31, 33, 41, 43, 50, 53
Mall, 66
Mallery, 55
Malvina, 21
Manda, 6
Mandy, 11
Mannall, 66
Manu, 2
Manuel, 1, 15, 21, 24, 42, 44
Mar, 60
Marcus, 39, 42, 46
Mareay, 66
Margaret, 3, 9, 19, 21, 36, 37, 41, 42, 49, 51, 57, 58, 59, 60
Marge, 31
Maria, 2, 3, 5, 6, 10, 12, 15, 16, 17, 18, 26, 29, 30, 31, 33, 36, 37, 38, 39, 40, 41, 43, 49, 51, 53, 54, 57, 59
Mariah, 4, 6, 20, 35, 52, 53
Mark, 21, 31
Mark Anthony, 31
MARLOW: Levi, 54; Mrs., 54; W.A., 54; Washington A., 52
Marshall, 3, 19, 21, 26, 40, 42, 44, 56, 58
Martha, 1, 5, 9, 20, 23, 27, 29, 31, 33, 37, 38, 39, 42, 43, 54, 59, 60
Martin, 1
Mary, 1, 3, 4, 6, 8, 9, 10, 11, 12, 14, 15, 16, 17, 18, 19, 20, 21, 22, 25, 27, 28, 29, 30, 31, 33, 35, 36, 37, 38, 39, 40, 41, 42, 43, 45, 46, 47, 49, 52, 55, 56, 57, 58, 59, 66
Mary Ann, 18, 25, 27, 28
Mary Eliza, 52, 60
Mary Frances, 47, 49
Mary Jane, 37, 49, 57
Mason, 57; Reuben, 3
MASSIE: Lewis D., 23, 29, 31
Matilda, 3, 8, 10, 12, 14, 15, 20, 21, 26, 31, 35, 36, 37, 46, 49, 53
Matt, 36
Matthew, 14
May, 6
May Louisa, 12
McDaniel, 49
McKAY: David, 33
McLATHAM: J., 36
McQUEEN: Boswell, 36; Cassandra, 36
Mela, 37
Melinda, 19, 39, 54
Melissa, 41
MELLON: Gobden S., 47
MENEFEE: Alexander F., 21; Alexander T., 59; Henry, 20; Henry R., 5; J.A., 39; James, 9, 10, 11, 13; James A., 24, 42; Lafayette S., 24; Philip S., 11; T.S., 28; Tabitha, 10, 11, 24, 28; William I., 59
Menor, 6
Menot, 6
Meredith, 7, 24
MEYERS: James H., 47
Middleton, 39, 43
Mildred, 5, 38, 51, 59
MILLAN: Francis, 60; H.F., 60; Henry F., 60; Sabina, 60
MILLER: B.F., 52, 55, 60; Franklin, 15; Henry, 55; Jane Grigsby, 53; Jesse, 55; John, 16, 37, 55; John M., 59; Polly, 15; William H., 41
MILLER B.T., 55
MILLER Sr.: John, 15
Millie, 57
Milly, 1, 3, 4, 6, 8, 10, 12, 15, 16, 17, 18, 19, 21, 22, 24, 25, 29, 33, 34, 37, 42, 43, 46, 59

Milton, 3, 44
Mima, 6, 21, 39
Mime, 4, 6
Miner, 6, 18
Minerva, 39
Minor, 17, 19, 24
Miranda, 13
Miriam, 30
Mishack, 50
MITCHELL: William, 61
Molly, 5, 53, 54, 55
MOORE: F., 60; George, 53; Henrietta, 51; James, 40; Lewis, 26, 27, 29; Maria, 40; Mary A., 61; Mary Ann, 53
Morgan, 13; Daniel, 11
MORRISON: Charlotte, 49; John A., 49; Mary A., 61; Mary F., 49; Russel, 49; Thomas Francis, 63
Morton, 39
Moses, 1, 2, 3, 4, 30, 43, 51, 52, 54, 57, 65
Moses Jr., 57
Mourning, 46
Muller: Zachariah, 65
Munroe, 12
MURPHY: Elias, 49; Jane, 49
MYERS: B.W., 35; Julian G., 45
N_as, 12
Nan, 66
Nancy, 2, 3, 6, 7, 8, 16, 19, 21, 22, 31, 36, 37, 40, 41, 42, 49
Narassa, 2
Nat, 3, 51
Nea, 57, 58
Ned, 12, 13, 21, 23, 24, 25, 30
Nelly, 3, 14, 21, 45, 51
Nelson, 1, 6, 8, 18, 19, 22, 26, 29, 39, 40, 41, 42
NELSON: Arthur, 21; James R., 15, 61; Sarah E., 60
NEWMAN: Alexander, 66; John, 66

NICOL: Michael, 14, 18
Nimrod, 43
Noah, 42, 46
NORMAN: Alcy, 1; Thomas, 1
Notley, 6
Nully, 3, 9, 10
OBANNON: Bryant, 25, 26; Charles Bryant, 25; Eliza, 25; J.M., 31; James, 25, 28; James M., 40, 42, 50; Jane, 25; John M., 25, 43; Joseph, 25; Lucy, 25; Mary, 25; Sarah, 25; Walt, 21; Walter, 25, 39
Ocean, 33
Ocsilin, 9
Olfilia, 41
Ophilia, 47
Orange, 39
Oscar, 8, 50, 51, 52, 57
Oswelo, 49
PAGE: Mary J., 44
PAINE: Anne, 66
Palmar, 66
PAR_LOW: Elisha, 21
PARR: James, 17
Pat, 29
Patience, 9
Patsy, 5, 21, 30, 58
Patty, 3, 7
PAYNE: Alexander, 12; Frances, 12; Frank, 12; George S., 12; James, 12; John, 12; Margaret E., 56; Patsy, 12; Robert, 64; Samuel, 12
Peg, 50
Peggy, 6, 9, 10, 50
Pendelton, 57
Pender, 33, 35
PENDLETON: George W., 18
PENN: John, 64
PERRY: Francis M., 33; William, 33
Pete, 66

Peter, 5, 6, 9, 19, 23, 27, 34, 39, 47, 49, 50, 56, 59, 65
PEYTON: Elizabeth, 41; Howard, 41; John, 41
Phil, 6, 12, 17, 18, 24
Philip, 3, 24, 31, 49
Phillis, 5, 6, 11, 13, 16, 17, 21, 25
Phoebe, 3, 39, 43
Phyllis, 1
PIERCE: Elizabeth Ann, 40
Polk, 57
Polly, 3, 7, 8, 18, 21, 34, 45, 49, 56
Pompey, 24, 25
POPHAM: Elizabeth Ann, 45; John N., 51; John W., 45
PORTER: Alcey, 4; John, 4, 6
Powell: John, 65
POWERS: James, 23; James L., 29
PRATT: Susan, 10; Susan Elizabeth Ann, 10; Thomas B., 10; William, 10
Presley, 25
PRIEST: Susan, 52
Primus, 51
Prince, 5, 6, 36
Priscilla, 29, 30, 55
Prudence, 3
PULLEN: Jesse, 56, 57; Nancy, 56
PULLER: Ann, 11, 17
PULLIN: Ann, 13
Rachel, 3, 8, 9, 10, 15, 20, 21, 49, 58
Ralph, 37
Randal, 14
Randall, 39, 42
Randol, 2
RAWLES: John, 55
RAWLINGS: Lucinda, 60
REAGEN: Henry, 35; Jacob, 34; John A., 34; Mary, 34
Rebecca, 2, 37, 41, 56

REID: Dr. Mark, 59; Joseph, 46
REID __ Mr., 45
Resin, 17
Reuben, 1, 2, 3, 4, 6, 7, 18, 21, 44, 50, 51, 52, 54
RHODES: Alfred D., 50; Arbelia, 53; Edward, 53
Rhody, 41
RICE: J.L., 47; John L., 50
Richard, 3, 6, 9, 10, 11, 12, 19, 35, 38, 43, 45, 46, 66
RICKETT: Hezekiah, 56; John C., 56
Ricksen: Lewis, 3
Rigen, 5
RISEY: Richard T., 17
Rison, 8
RITENOUR: David, 21, 27
RIVERCOMB: William, 47
ROBERSON: William, 54
Robert, 3, 8, 10, 13, 14, 15, 16, 17, 26, 29, 39, 40, 55, 58, 65
Roberta, 49
ROBERTS: William H., 27
ROBERTSON: Elizabeth, 8; Rose, 8; William Mitchell, 8
ROBERTSON Sr.: Elijah, 9; Mitchell, 8
Robin, 14, 20, 21
Robinson, 1
ROBINSON: Elizabeth, 26; Mary, 9
ROMINE: John, 59
Rosaline, 19
Rosanna, 3
Rose, 8, 9, 10, 11, 23, 39, 41, 53, 54
Rosella, 38
Rosetta, 17
Rosette, 15
Rousey, 22
ROWLES: B.F., 53
Roxaline, 24, 30, 49
Roy, 6, 52, 54
ROYSTON: John T., 30

RUDASELLA: Jale, 26
RUDASILL: Phillip, 13
RUDASILLA: Richard L., 52
Russel, 33
Russell, 37
Ruth, 35
Ruthy, 5, 57
Sabra, 8
Sally, 1, 5, 9, 10, 14, 16, 21, 28, 30, 38, 39, 41, 42, 43, 45, 46, 51, 53, 55, 56, 60
Sam, 1, 2, 3, 7, 9, 18, 21, 22, 42, 50
Samuel, 2, 3, 4, 19, 26, 51
Sandy, 3, 40, 41, 44
Sanford, 1, 16, 55; Judy, 3
Sarah, 5, 9, 10, 16, 19, 21, 29, 33, 34, 36, 37, 38, 45, 47, 49, 53, 54
Sarah Ann, 50, 51, 52, 53, 54
Sarah Catharine, 53
Sarah Catherine, 21
Sarah Virginia, 23
Sary, 2
SAUNDERS: Katharine A., 26; Mildred, 45, 46
Saw, 66
Sawney, 21, 41, 42
Sawny, 43
Scott, 58
SCOTT: Elizabeth Lane, 22; Fanny, 42; John, 51; John F., 41; M. Frances, 22; Martha F., 41, 42; Samuel, 65; William, 15
SEARS: Mary Catharine, 56
SEAVELL: Benjamin D., 42; John M., 42
SEDWICK: Benjamin, 35; Elizabeth, 35, 37, 38; Elvira, 35; George W., 36; James B., 35, 52; Malinda F., 36; Mary, 52; William H., 35, 40; Zadock, 35
Selas, 59

Seniora, 65
Sephrona, 22
Seth, 51, 53
SETTLE: Agnes, 29; Dinnah, 13; Elijah, 18, 22; Elizabeth, 15, 55, 60; Ephram, 14; Francis, 60; Franklin, 15; Henry, 15; John, 15; John J., 55; Marryman, 13; Turner, 44
Shack, 50
Shadrach, 54
Shelton: George, 51
Shubel, 7
Shumate: Charlotte, 6
Sidney, 53
Silar, 57
Silas, 31
SILLARD: William J., 52
SILMAN: Landon, 60
Silvey, 2, 22
Silvy, 16, 18, 43
SIMMS: Abner, 46
Simon, 6, 8
SIMPSON: Elizabeth, 3
SIMS: Abner, 45; Martha A., 60
Sinah, 7
SINGLETON: A.J., 60; Jane, 58
SLAUGHTER: Eliza L., 42; Francis, 63; Montgomery, 42; Reuben, 58; Robert, 18
SLOAN: Mary, 34
SLOANE: James, 45, 46, 53
Smith, 38
SMITH: Charles, 52; Cornelius, 50; John, 9, 10; Lucy M. Obannon, 50; O.P., 21; S.C., 46; Sarah C., 45, 53; Sophia, 45; Thomas, 10; William, 10, 36, 37
SMITH Sr.: Delphia, 10
SMITHER: Mrs. Getty, 21
Solomon, 6, 11, 16, 18, 22

Somerfield, 37
Somerville, 10, 15, 21, 38, 39
Sooky, 51
Sophia, 2, 4, 19, 49, 53
SPARKS: H.T., 37; Henry, 53
Spencer, 23
SPILLER: Elizabeth, 22; Tamar, 22
SPINDLE: Adelene A., 11; Col. Thomas, 15; Eliza V., 26, 29; John P., 20; Thomas, 19; William A., 11, 19, 20
Squire, 2, 4, 44
STALLARD: Susannah, 11
Stephen, 3, 5, 8, 9, 13, 33, 40, 41
Stephney, 35
Stepney, 33
STOLLAND: James, 12
Stowe: Jane, 65
STRINGFELLOW: Benjamin, 59, 60; Susannah, 59
Strother, 9, 10, 17, 18, 23, 37, 52, 53
Stuart, 25
Sucky, 1
Summerville, 17
Sunderland: Rebs_a, 63
SURNDLIN: A.C., 55
Susan, 3, 17, 19, 21, 24, 25, 29, 33, 34, 37, 39, 42, 51
Susan_, 3
Susana, 66
Suzanna, 66
SWINDLER: Ellen, 34, 38; Henry, 35, 36
Szdno, 49
Tabitha, 59
TACKETT: Jainel, 64
Talby, 14
Taliafero, 18, 22, 44
Tamey, 36
TANCIL: Francis, 25
TANNEHILL: William, 55
Tanner, 2

TAPP: Dicy, 38; Judith, 15; Vincent, 15
TAYLOR: Richard, 66
Tel, 4
Tell, 6
Temple, 23
Tender, 12
Teresy, 9
Terry, 26
Theodosia, 34
Thom, 55, 59
Thomas, 2, 4, 5, 13, 16, 17, 21, 26, 30, 37, 49, 51, 57, 64, 65, 66
Thompson, 19
THOMPSON: Caroline H., 1
THORNHILL: Bryant, 12; Joseph, 12; Richard, 39, 53; Robert, 12; Thomas, 12; William, 12
Thornton, 2, 3, 5, 6, 18, 22, 24, 27, 33, 34, 37, 40, 49, 51, 52, 57
THORNTON: Alfred A., 1; Aylell W., 1; Charles A., 7; Elizabeth A.T., 1, 5; George W., 1; Howard, 2; Jane, 1, 5; Mary Frances, 1, 5; Philip, 43
THROOP: Harriet C., 20
Tilda, 18
Till, 53
TIMBERLAKE: Richard H., 38
Toby, 66
Toliver, 29; Tom, 3
Tom, 3, 6, 7, 8, 11, 14, 18, 19, 21, 22, 24, 25, 33, 35, 65
Tompson, 2
Tuck, 59
TURLEY, 38; Charles, 57; Nancy, 34, 58
Turner, 11, 21, 31, 55, 59
TURNER: Anna, 29; Jane Maria, 29; John Robert, 29; Lewis, 29; Martha, 9; Susan, 29; Zephaniah, 29

Umphry, 53
UPDIKE: Daniel, 21; Hannah, 24; John, 31, 33; Mrs. Ury, 33
UPDIKE Sr.: Daniel, 24
Uriah, 36, 37
VANHORN: Jesse, 61
Venus, 9
Vina, 40, 51
Vincent, 2
Violet, 12, 26
Violette, 57
Virginia, 57
Wagonam, 36
Walden, 6
WALDEN: Carnot M., 30; Lucy, 30; Thomas, 3, 29; William, 28; William M., 30
Walker, 3, 12, 17, 19, 20; Sally, 3
WALKER: Easter, 66; Elizabeth, 66; Frances, 66; Jane, 66; Sarah, 66
Wallace, 58
WALTER: Harriet G., 54
Warner, 16, 31, 33
Warren, 16
Warrenton, 3, 21
Washington, 2, 4, 7, 12, 19, 21, 27, 39
WATERS: Ann, 16; C.T., 28; John, 14; Jonathan, 16; Mortimore, 14; Sandy, 14; Sandy P., 14; William, 28
Watts: Betty, 66
Welford, 17
Wesley, 1, 22, 37
WHEATLEY: Sarah, 15, 55
Wheden, 53
WHITE: Sarah Ann, 8
WHITESCARVER: Frances, 50; L.C., 50; R.A., 50; Winston P., 57
Whiting: William, 3

WHITLOCK: Anthony, 66; James, 66; John, 66; Thomas, 66
Will, 14, 20, 29, 66
WILLET: George, 11; Sarah, 11
Willey, 49
WILLEY: Edward, 7
William, 1, 3, 4, 5, 9, 10, 16, 25, 27, 30, 31, 33, 37, 38, 39, 42, 45, 46, 49, 52, 58, 59
Williamson, 14
WILLIAMSON: Henry, 64
Willis, 4, 5, 6, 7, 36, 47
WILLIS: Charles, 12
Wilson, 13; John, 51
WILSON: Eveline, 53; Isaac, 35; Jamima Jane, 35; Maria, 49, 53; Washington, 53
Winfried, 12
Winney, 5, 9, 10, 17, 21, 34, 52, 54, 56, 58
Winney, 27
WITHERS: Catherine, 6; Catherine Hillary, 36; Frances, 6; James, 4; Susan, 6
WITHERS Jr.: James, 2
WITHERS Sr.: James, 6, 10
WOOD: Burwell K., 12, 27; John H., 20; Lewis, 8; Lucy, 15, 55; Mary A., 61; Mrs., 55
WOODARD: Albert C., 28; James M., 45, 50
WOODBRIDGE: Paule, 66
Woodson, 21, 38, 42, 46
WOODWELL: Burr, 24
WRIGHT: Mary, 63; Thomas, 63
YAGER: William, 21
YATES: Besy, 15; Charles, 53
Zachariah, 65
Zilphey, 46
Zoliver: Esther, 3

www.ingramcontent.com/pod-product-compliance
Lightning Source LLC
Chambersburg PA
CBHW050844160426
43192CB00011B/2140